March of America Facsimile Series

Number 21

Journall of the English Plantation at Plimoth

Journall of the English Plantation at Plimoth

ANN ARBOR

UNIVERSITY MICROFILMS, INC.

A Subsidiary of Xerox Corporation

Foreword

A Relation Or Iournall of the beginning and proceedings of the English Plantation settled at Plimoth in New England, printed in London in 1622, was the first published account of the voyage of the Pilgrims to New England and of their settlement at Plymouth. Although the general outline of the story is a familiar one to Americans, it has become encrusted through the years with successive layers of legend and myth. Here, then, is the history of the Pilgrim landing told by those who were present.

The principal narrative describes the voyage of the "Mayflower," the first Pilgrim explorations ashore, and the construction of a permanent settlement at Plymouth. It explains the circumstances surrounding the signing of the "Mayflower Compact" for the future government of the colony. "This day before we came to harbour, observing some not well affected to unitie and concord, but gave some appearance of faction, it was thought good there should be an association and agreement...to submit to such government and governours, as we should by common censent agree to make and chose." The narrative makes frequent references to the hardships endured by the Pilgrims during their first winter in America. The rigors of the climate "brought to the most, if not to all, coughes and colds...whereof many dyed."

A "letter" contained in this edition describes the better days which were to come, however. With the harvest in, the Pilgrims arranged a celebration of thanksgiving "that so we might after a more speciall manner reioyce together, after we had gathered the fruit of our labours." Many of the Indians joined them, "and amongst the rest their greatest King Massasoyt with some nintie men." Other descriptions of Pilgrim activity reveal the generally good *rapport* which they had established with the Indians. Also of interest are the arguments given to justify abandoning homes in the old world for settlement in the new world. These arguments were aimed with obvious intent at prospective colonists in England. To those in England already preparing to come to Plymouth, the book offered practical advice. Among other things, the future colonists were counseled to "bring good store of clothes, and beding with you; bring every man a Musket or fowling Peece."

This collection of material about the Plymouth Colony is often referred to as "Mourt's Relation." The name G. Mourt (Morton) does appear at the end of the preface to the reader, but it is generally believed that he simply arranged for publication in London. William Bradford and Edward Winslow, present on the first voyage, are those whose names are usually attached to some of these pieces. John Smith abstracted much of this material for inclusion in his *Generall Historie* of 1624. In 1625 Samuel Purchas also inserted a condensed version of the book in his *Pilgrimes*. The English public therefore had considerable opportunity to become acquainted with the colony at Plymouth. For additional information, see the introduction of Dwight B. Heath in his edition of *A Journal of the Pilgrims at Plymouth* (New York, 1963), pp. vii-xvii, and the introduction of Henry M. Dexter to his edition of *Mourt's Relation or Journal of the Plantation at Plymouth* (Boston, 1865), pp. xi-xxxi.

Journall of the English Plantation at Plimoth

A RELATION OR

Iournall of the beginning and proceedings of the Englifh Plantation fetled at *Plimoth* in NEW ENGLAND, by certaine Englifh Aduenturers both Merchants and others.

With their difficult paffage, their fafe ariuall, their ioyfull building of, and comfortable planting themfelues in the now well defended Towne of NEW PLIMOTH.

AS ALSO A RELATION OF FOVRE feuerall difcoueries fince made by fome of the fame Englifh Planters there refident.

I. In a iourney to PVCKANOKICK *the habitation of the Indians greateft King* Maffafoyt : *as alfo their meffage, the anfwer and entertainment they had of him.*

II. In a voyage made by ten of them to the Kingdome of Nawfet, *to feeke a boy that had loft himfelfe in the woods : with fuch accidents as befell them in that voyage.*

III. In their iourney to the Kingdome of Namafchet, *in defence of their greateft King* Maffafoyt, *againft the* Narrohigganfets, *and to reuenge the fuppofed death of their Interpreter* Tifquantum.

IIII. Their voyage to the Maffachufets, *and their entertainment there.*

With an anfwer to all fuch obiections as are any way made againft the lawfulneffe of Englifh plantations in thofe parts.

LONDON,

Printed for *Iohn Bellamie*, and are to be fold at his fhop at the two

S.ʳ Thomas Hanmer of Hanmer
in Com: Flint Baronet 1707

To the Reader.

Ourteous *Reader*, *be intreated to make a favorable conſtruction of my forwardnes, in publiſhing theſe inſeuing diſcourſes, the deſire of carrying the Goſpell of Chriſt, into thoſe forraigne parts, amongſt thoſe people that as yet haue had no knowledge, nor taſt of God, as alſo to procure vnto themſelues and others a quiet and comfortable habytation : weare amongſt other things the inducements (vnto theſe vndertakers of the then hopefull, and now experimentally knowne good enterprice for plantation, in New England, to ſet afoote and proſecute the ſame & though it fared with them, as it is common to the moſt actions of this nature, that the firſt at-temps proue diffecult, as the ſequell more at large expreſſeth, yet it hath pleaſed God, euē beyond our expectation in ſo ſhort a time, to giue hope of let-ting ſome of them ſee (though ſome he hath taken out of this vale of teares) ſome grounds of hope, of the acccompliſhment of both thoſe endes by them, at firſt propounded.*

And as my ſelfe then much deſired, and ſhort-

ly

To the Reader.

ly hope to effect, if the Lord will the putting to of
my shoulder in this hopefull businesse, and in the
meane time, these relations comming to my hand
from my both known & faithful friends, on whose
writings I do much rely, I thought it not a misse to
make them more generall, hoping of a cheerefull
proceeding, both of Aduenturers and planters, in=
treating that the example of the hon: Virginia
and Bermudas Companies, incountering with so
many distasters, and that for diuers yeares toge=
ther, with an vnwearied resolution, the good ef=
fects whereof are now eminent, may preuaile as a
spurre of preparation also touching this no lesse
hopefull Country though yet an infant, the extent
& comodities whereof are as yet not fully known,
after time wil vnfould more: such as desire to take
knowledge of things, may in forme themselues by
this insuing treatise, and if they please also by such
as haue bin there a first and second time, my har-
ty prayer to God is that the euent of this and all
other honorable and honest vndertakings, may be
for the furtherance of the kingdome of Christ, the
inlarging of the bounds of our Soueraigne Lord
King Iames, & the good and profit of those, who
either by purse, or person, or both, are agents in
the same, so I take leaue and rest

Thy friend, G. M o v r t.

CERTAINE VSEFVL
ADVERTISEMENTS SENT
in a Letter written by a difcreete friend vnto the Planters in *New England*, at their firft fetting
faile from Southhampton, *who earneftly defireth*
the profperitie of that their new
Plantation.

* *
*

Ouing and Chriftian friends, I doe
heartily and in the Lord falute you
all, as being they with whom I am
prefent in my beft affection, and moft
earneft longings after you, though I
be conftrained for a while to be bodily abfent from
you, I fay conftrained, God knowing how willingly and much rather then otherwife I would haue
haue borne my part with you in this firft brunt,
were I not by ftrong neceffitie held backe for the
prefent. Make account of me in the meane while,
as of a man deuided in my felfe with great paine,
and as (naturall bonds fet afide) hauing my better
part with you. And though I doubt not but in
your godly wifedomes you both forefee and re-
folue vpon that which concerneth your prefent

ſtate and condition both ſeuerally and ioyntly, yet
haue I thought but my dutie to adde ſome further
ſpurre of prouocation vnto them who run already,
if not becauſe you need it, yet becauſe I owe it in
loue and dutie.

And firſt, as we are daily to renew our repentance
with our God, ſpeciall for our ſinnes knowne, and
generall for our vnknowne treſpaſſes; ſo doth the
Lord call vs in a ſingular maner vpon occaſions of
ſuch difficultie and danger as lieth vpon you, to a
both more narrow ſearch and carefull reformation
of our wayes in his ſight, leſt he calling to remem-
brance our ſinnes forgotten by vs or vnrepented of,
take aduantage againſt vs, and in iudgement leaue
vs for the ſame to be ſwallowed vp in one danger
or other; whereas on the contrary, ſin being taken
away by earneſt repentance and the pardon thereof
from the Lord, ſealed vp vnto a mans conſcience
by his Spirit, great ſhall be his ſecuritie and peace
in all dangers, ſweete his comforts in all diſtreſſes,
with happie deliuerance from all euill, whether in
life or in death.

Now next after this heauenly peace with God
and our owne conſciences, we are carefully to pro-
uide for peace with all men what in vs lieth, eſpecially with our aſſociates, and for that end watchful-
nes muſt be had, that we neither at all in our ſelues
do giue, no nor eaſily take offence being giuen by
others. Woe be vnto the world for offences, for
though it be neceſſary (conſidering the malice of
Satan and mans corruption) that offences come,
yet woe vnto the man or woman either by whom
the

the offence cometh, faith Chrift, Math. 18. 7. And if offences in the vnfeafonable vfe of things in them felues indifferent, be more to be feared then death it felfe, as the Apoftle teacheth, 1. Cor. 9. 15. how much more in things fimply euill, in which neither honour of God nor loue of man is thought worthy to be regarded.

Neither yet is it fufficient that we keep our felues by the grace of God from giuing offence, except withall we be armed againft the taking of them when they are giuen by others. For how vnperfect and lame is the worke of grace in that perfon, who wants charitie to couer a multitude of offences, as the Scriptures fpeake. Neither are you to be exhorted to this grace onely vpon the common grounds of Chriftianitie, which are, that perfons ready to take offence, either want charitie to couer offences, or wifedome duly to weigh humane frailtie; or laftly are groffe, though clofe hypocrites, as Chrift our Lord teacheth, Math. 7. 1, 2, 3. as indeed in mine owne experience, few or none haue beene found which fooner giue offence, then fuch as eafily take it; neither haue they euer proued found and profitable members in focieties, which haue nourifhed in themfelues that touchey humour. But befides thefe, there are diuers fpetiall motiues prouoking you aboue others to great care and confcience this way: As firft, you are many of you ftrangers, as to the perfons, fo to the infirmities one of another, and fo ftand in neede of more watchfulneffe this way, left when fuch things fall out in men and women as you fufpected not, you be inordinately affected with them; which doth require at your hands much wisedome and charitie for the couering and preuenting of incident offences that way. And lastly your intended course of ciuill communitie wil minister continuall occasion of offence, and will be as fuell for that fire, except you diligently quench it with brotherly forbearance. And if taking of offence causlesly or easily at mens doings be so carefully to be auoided, how much more heed is to be taken that we take not offence at God himselfe, which yet we certainly do so oft as we do murmure at his prouidence in our crosses, or beare impatiently such afflictions as wherewith he pleaseth to visit vs. Store we vp therefore patience against the euill day, without which we take offence at the Lord himselfe in his holy and iust works.

A fourth thing there is carefully to be prouided for, to wit, that with your common emploiments you ioyne common affections truly bent vpon the generall good, auoiding as a deadly plague of your both common and speciall comfort all retirednesse of minde for proper aduantage, and all singularly affected any maner of way; let euery man represse in himselfe and the whole bodie in each person, as so many rebels against the common good, all priuate respects of mens selues, not sorting with the generall conueniencie. And as men are carefull not to haue a new house shaken with any violence before it be well settled and the parts firmly knit: so be you, I beseech you brethren, much more carefull, that the house of God which you are and are

to

to be, be not fhaken with vnneceſſary noueltics or other oppofitions at the firſt fettling thereof.

Laſtly, whereas you are to become a body politik, vfing amongſt your felues ciuill gouernment, and are not furnifhed with any perfons of fpeciall eminencie abouę the reſt, to be chofen by you into office of gouernment: Let your witedome and godlineſſe appeare, not onely in chufing fuch perfons as do entirely loue, and will diligently promote the common good, but alſo in yeelding vnto them all due honour and obedience in their lawfull adminiſtrations; not beholding in them the ordinarineſſe of their perfons, but Gods ordinance for your good; nor being like vnto the foolifh multitude, who more honour the gay coate, then either the vertuous mind of the man, or glorious ordinance of the Lord. But you know better things, and that the image of the Lords power and authoritie which the Magiſtrate beareth, is honorable, in how meane perfons foeuer. And this dutie you both may the more willingly, and ought the more confcionably to performe, becauſe you are at leaſt for the prefent to haue onely them for your ordinary gouernours, which your felues fhall make choiſe of for that worke.

Sundrie other things of importance I could put you in mind of, and of thoſe before mentioned in more words, but I will not ſo far wrong your godly minds, as to thinke you heedleſſe of theſe things, there being alſo diuers among you fo well able to admonifh both themfelues and others of what concerneth them. Theſe few things therefore, and
the

the same in few words I do earnestly commend vnto your care and conscience, ioyning therewith my
daily incessant prayers vnto the Lord, that he who
hath made the heauens and the earth, the sea and
all riuers of waters, and whose prouidence is ouer
all his workes, especially ouer all his deare children
for good, would so guide and guard you in your
wayes, as inwardly by his Spirit, so outwardly by
the hand of his power, as that both you and we also, for and with you, may haue after matter of prai-
sing his Name all the days of your and our liues.
Fare you well in him in whom you trust, and in
whom I rest

An vnfained well-willer
of your happie successe
in this hopefull voyage,

I. R.

TO HIS MVCH RE-
spected *Friend,* M^r. *I. P.*

Ood Friend : As wee cannot but account it an extraordinary bleſſing of God in directing our courſe for theſe parts, after we came out of our natiue countrey, for that we had the happineſſe to be poſſeſſed of the comforts we receiue by the benefit of one of the moſt pleaſant, moſt healthfull, and moſt fruitfull parts of the world: So muſt wee acknowledge the ſame bleſſing to bee multiplied vpon our whole company, for that we obtained the honour to receiue allowance and approbation of our free poſſeſſion, and enioying thereof vnder the authority of thoſe thrice honoured Perſons, the *Preſident* and *Counſell* for the affaires of *New-England,* by whoſe bounty and grace, in that behalfe, all of vs are tied to dedicate our beſt ſeruice vnto them, as thoſe vnder his Majeſtie, that wee owe it vnto: whoſe noble endeuours in theſe their

A 3   actions

actions the God of heauen and earth multiply to his glory and their owne eternall comforts.

As for this poore Relation, I pray you to accept it, as being writ by the seuerall Actors themselues, after their plaine and rude manner; therefore doubt nothing of the truth thereof: if it be defectiue in any thing, it is their ignorance, that are better acquainted with planting then writing. If it satisfie those that are well affected to the businesse, it is all I care for. Sure I am the place we are in, and the hopes that are apparent, cannot but suffice any that will not desire more then enough, neither is there want of ought among vs but company to enioy the blessings so plentifully bestowed vpon the inhabitants that are here. While I was a writing this, I had almost forgot, that I had but the recommendation of the relation it selfe, to your further consideration, and therefore I will end without saying more, saue that I shall alwaies rest

From PLIMOTH in
New-England.

Yours in the way of
friendship, R. G.

A RELATION OR
IOVRNALL OF THE
PROCEEDINGS OF THE
Plantation fetled at *Plimoth* in
New ENGLAND.

Ednefday the fixt of *September*, the Wind comming Eaft North Eaft, a fine fmall gale, we loofed from *Plimoth*, hauing beene kindly intertained and curteoufly vfed by diuers friends there dwelling, and after many difficulties in boyfterous ftormes, at length by Gods prouidence vpon the ninth of *Nouember* following, by breake of the day we efpied land which we deemed to be *Cape Cod*, and fo afterward it proued. And the appearance of it much comforted vs, efpecially, feeing fo goodly a Land, and woodded to the brinke of the fea, it caufed vs to reioyce together, and praife God that had giuen vs once againe to fee land. And thus wee made our courfe South South Weft, purpofing to goe to a Riuer ten leagues

to

to the South of the Cape, but at night the winde being contrary, we put round againe for the Bay of *Cape Cod* : and vpon the 11. of *Nouember*, we came to an anchor in the Bay, which is a good harbour and pleasant Bay, circled round, except in the entrance, which is about foure miles ouer from land to land, compassed about to the very Sea with Okes, Pines, Iuniper, Sassafras, and other sweet wood; it is a harbour wherein 1000. saile of Ships may safely ride, there we relieued our selues with wood and water, and refreshed our people, while our shallop was fitted to coast the Bay, to search for an habitation : there was the greatest store of fowle that euer we saw.

And euery day we saw Whales playing hard by vs, of which in that place, if we had instruments & meanes to take them, we might haue made a very rich returne, which to our great griefe we wanted. Our master and his mate, and others experienced in fishing, professed, we might haue made three or foure thousand pounds worth of Oyle; they preferred it before Greenland Whale-fishing, & purpose the next winter to fish for Whale here ; for Cod we assayed, but found none, there is good store no doubt in their season. Neither got we any fish all the time we lay there, but some few little ones on the shore. We found great Mussles, and very fat and full of Sea pearle, but we could not eat them, for they made vs all sicke that did eat, as well saylers as passengers ; they caused to cast and scoure, but they were soone well againe. The bay is so round & circling, that before we could come to anchor, we went round all the points of the Compasse. We could not come neere the shore by three quarters of an English mile, because of shallow water, which was a great preiudice to vs, for our people going on shore were forced to wade a bow shoot or two in going aland, which caused many to get colds and coughs, for it was many times freezing cold weather.

This day before we came to harbour, obseruing some not well affected to vnitie and concord, but gaue some appearance of faction, it was thought good there should be an association and agreement, that we should combine together
in

in one body, and to submit to such government and governours, as we should by common consent agree to make and chose, and set our hands to this that followes word for word.

IN the name of God, Amen. We whose names are vnderwritten, the loyall Subiects of our dread soveraigne Lord King IAMES, by the grace of God of Great *Britaine, France,* and *Ireland* King, Defender of the Faith, &c.

Having vnder-taken for the glory of God, and advancement of the Christian Faith, and honour of our King and Countrey, a Voyage to plant the first Colony in the Northerne parts of VIRGINIA, doe by these presents solemnly & mutually in the presence of *God* and one of another, covenant, and combine our selues together into a civill body politike, for our better ordering and preservation, and furtherance of the ends aforesaid; and by vertue hereof to enact, constitute, and frame such iust and equall Lawes, Ordinances, acts, constitutions, offices from time to time, as shall be thought most meet and convenient for the generall good of the Colony: vnto which we promise all due submission and obedience. In witnesse whereof we haue here vnder subscribed our names. *Cape Cod* 11. of *November,* in the yeare of the raigne of our soveraigne Lord King IAMES, of *England, France,* and *Ireland* 18. and of *Scotland* 54. *Anno Domino* 1620.

The same day so soone as we could we set a-shore 15. or 16. men, well armed, with some to fetch wood, for we had none left; as also to see what the Land was, and what Inhabitants they could meet with, they found it to be a small neck of Land; on this side where we lay is the *Bay*, and the further side the Sea; the ground or earth, sand hils, much like the Downes in *Holland,* but much better; the crust of the earth a Spits depth, excellent blacke earth; all wooded with Okes, Pines, Sassafras, Iuniper, Birch, Holly, Vines, some Ash, Walnut; the wood for the most part open and without vnderwood, fit either to goe or ride in: at night our people returned

C 2

ned, but found not any perfon, nor habitation, and laded
their Boat with Iuniper, which fmelled very fweet & ftrong,
and of which we burnt the moft part of the time we lay
there.

Munday the 13. of *November*, we vnfhipped our Shallop
and drew her on land, to mend and repaire her, having bin
forced to cut her downe in beftowing her betwixt the
decks, and fhe was much opened with the peoples lying in
her, which kept vs long there, for it was 16.or 17.dayes before the Carpenter had finifhed her ; our people went on
fhore to refrefh themfelues, and our women to wafh, as they
had great need ; but whileft we lay thus ftill, hoping our
Shallop would be ready in fiue or fixe dayes at the furtheft,
but our Carpenter made flow worke of it, fo that fome of
our people impatient of delay, defired for our better furtherance to travaile by Land into the Countrey, which was not
without appearance of danger, not having the Shallop with
them, nor meanes to carry provifion, but on their backes, to
fee whether it might be fit for vs to feate in or no, and the rather becaufe as we fayled into the Harbour, there feemed to
be a river opening it felfe into the maine land; the willingnes
of the perfous was liked, but the thing it felfe, in regard of
the danger was rather permitted then approved, and fo with
cautions, directions, and inftructions, fixteene men were
fet out with every man his Musket, Sword, and Corflet, vnder the conduct of Captaine *Miles Standifh*, vnto whom was
adioyned for counfell and advife, *William Bradford, Stephen
Hopkins*, and *Edward Tilley*.

Wednefday the 15. of *November*, they were fet a fhore,
and when they had ordered themfelues in the order of a fingle File, and marched about the fpace of a myle, by the Sea
they efpyed fiue or fixe people, with a Dogge, comming towards them, who were Savages, who when they faw them
ran into the Wood and whiftled the Dogge after them, &c.
Firft, they fuppofed them to be mafter *Iones*, the Mafter and
fome of his men, for they were a fhore, and knew of their
comming, but after they knew them to be *Indians* they marched

ched after them into the Woods, least other of the *Indians*
should lie in Ambush ; but when the *Indians* saw our men following them, they ran away with might and mayne, and our
men turned out of the Wood after them, for it was the way
they intended to goe, but they could not come neare them.
They followed them that night about ten miles by the trace
of their footings, and saw how they had come the same way
they went, and at a turning perceived how they run vp an
hill, to see whether they followed them. At length night
came vpon them, and they were constrained to take vp their
lodging, so they set forth three Sentinells, and the rest, some
kindled a fire, and others fetched wood, and there held our
Randevous that night. In the morning so soone as we could
see the trace, we proceeded on our iourney, & had the tracke
vntill we had compassed the head of a long creake, and there
they tooke into another wood, and we after them, supposing
to finde some of their dwellings, but we marched thorow
boughes and bushes, and vnder hills and vallies, which tore
our very Armour in peeces, and yet could meete with none
of them, nor their houses, nor finde any fresh water, which
we greatly desired, and stood in need off, for we brought
neither Beere nor Water with vs, and our victuals was onely Bisket and Holland cheese, and a little Bottle of *aquavite*,
so as we were sore a thirst. About ten a clocke we came into
a deepe Valley, full of brush, wood-gaile, and long grasse,
through which we found little paths or tracts, and there we
saw a Deere, and found springs of fresh water, of which we
were heartily glad, and sat vs downe and drunke our first
New-England water with as much delight as euer we drunke
drinke in all our liues. When we had refreshed our selues,
we directed our course full South, that we might come to the
shore, which within a short while after we did, and there
made a fire, that they in the ship might see where wee were
(as we had direction) and so marched on towards this supposed River ; and as we went in another valley, we found
a fine cleere Pond of fresh water, being about a Musket shot
broad, and twise as long ; there grew also many small vines,

and

and Foule and Deere haunted there ; there grew much Safa-
fras : from thence we went on & found much plaine ground,
about fiftie Acres, fit for the Plow, and some signes where the
Indians had formerly planted their corne ; after this, some
thought it best for nearenesse of the river to goe downe and
travaile on the Sea sands, by which meanes some of our men
were tyred, and lagged behind, so we stayed and gathered
them vp, and struck into the Land againe ; where we found a
little path to certaine heapes of sand, one whereof was covered with old Matts, and had a woodden thing like a morter
whelmed on the top of it, and an earthen pot layd in a little
hole at the end thereof; we musing what it might be, digged
& found a Bow, and, as we thought, Arrowes, but they were
rotten ; We supposed there were many other things, but
because we deemed them graues, we put in the Bow againe
and made it vp as it was, and left the rest vntouched, because
we thought it would be odious vnto them to ransacke their
Sepulchers. We went on further and found new stubble, of
which they had gotten Corne this yeare, and many Wallnut
trees full of Nuts, and great store of Strawberries, and some
Vines ; passing thus a field or two, which were not great, we
came to another, which had also bin new gotten, and there
we found where an house had beene, and foure or fiue old
Plankes layed together ; also we found a great Ketle, which
had beene some Ships ketle and brought out of *Europe*; there
was also an heape of sand, made like the former, but it was
newly done, we might see how they had padled it with their
hands, which we digged vp, and in it we found a little old
Basket full of faire *Indian* Corne, and digged further & found
a fine great new Basket full of very faire corne of this yeare,
with some 36. goodly eares of corne, some yellow, and some
red, and others mixt with blew, which was a very goodly
sight : the Basket was round, and narrow at the top, it held
about three or foure Bushels, which was as much as two of vs
could lift vp from the ground, and was very handsomely
and cunningly made ; But whilst wee were busie about these
things, we set our men Sentinell in a round ring, all but two

or

or three which digged vp the corne. We were in ſuſpence,
what to doe with it, and the Ketle, and at length after much
conſultation, we concluded to take the Ketle, and as much
of the Corne as we could carry away with vs ; and when our
Shallop came, if we could find any of the people, and come
to parley with them, we would giue them the Ketle againe,
and ſatisfie them for their Corne, ſo wee tooke all the eares
and put a good deale of the looſe Corne in the Ketle for two
men to bring away on a ſtaffe ; beſides, they that could put
any into their Pockets filled the ſame ; the reſt wee buried a-
gaine, for we were ſo laden with Armour that we could carry no more. Not farre from this place we found the remain-
der of an old Fort, or Palizado, which as we conceiued had
beene made by ſome Chriſtians, this was alſo hard by that
place which we thought had beene a river, vnto which wee
went and found it ſo to be, deviding it ſelfe into two armes
by an high banke, ſtanding right by the cut or mouth which
came from the Sea, that which was next vnto vs was the leſſe,
the other arme was more then twiſe as big, and not vnlike to
be an harbour for ſhips ; but whether it be a freſh river, or
onely an indraught of the Sea, we had no time to diſcover ;
for wee had Commandement to be out but two dayes. Here
alſo we ſaw two Canoas, the one on the one ſide, the other
on the other ſide, wee could not beleeue it was a Canoa, till
we came neare it, ſo we returned leauing the further diſco-
very hereof to our Shallop, and came that night backe againe
to the freſh water pond, and there we made our Randevous
that night, making a great fire, and a Baricado to windward
of vs, and kept good watch with three Sentinells all night,
euery one ſtanding when his turne came, while fiue or ſixe
inches of Match was burning. It proved a very rainie night.
In the morning we tooke our Ketle and ſunke it in the pond,
and trimmed our Muskets, for few of them would goe off
becauſe of the wett, and ſo coaſted the wood againe to come
home, in which we were ſhrewdly puſ-led, and loſt our way,
as we wandred we came to a tree, where a yong Spritt was
bowed downe over a bow, and ſome Acornes ſtrewed vnder it

der neath; *Stephen Hopkins* sayd, it had beene to catch some Deere, so, as we were looking at it, *William Bradford* being in the *Reare*, when he came looked also vpon it, and as he went about, it gaue a sodaine jerk vp, and he was immediately caught by the leg; It was a very pretie deuise, made with a Rope of their owne making, and hauing a noose as artificially made, as any Roper in *England* can make, and as like ours as can be, which we brought away with vs. In the end wee got out of the Wood, and were fallen about a myle too high aboue the creake, where we saw three Bucks, but we had rather haue had one of them. Wee also did spring three couple of Partridges; and as we came along by the creake, wee saw great flockes of wild Geese and Duckes, but they were very fearefull of vs. So we marched some while in the Woods, some while on the sands, and other while in the water vp to the knees, till at length we came neare the Ship, and then we shot off our Peeces, and the long Boat came to fetch vs; master *Iones*, and master *Caruer* being on the shore, with many of our people, came to meete vs. And thus wee came both weary and well-come home, and deliuered in our Corne into the store, to be kept for seed, for wee knew not how to come by any, and therefore were very glad, purposing so soone as we could meete with any of the Inhabitants of that place, to make them large satisfaction. This was our first Discovery, whilst our Shallop was in repairing; our people did make things as fitting as they could, and time would, in seeking out wood, and heluing of Tooles, and sawing of Tymber to build a new Shallop, but the discommodiousnes of the harbour did much hinder vs, for we could neither gee to, nor come from the shore, but at high water, which was much to our hinderance and hurt, for oftentimes they waded to the midle of the thigh, and oft to the knees, to goe and come from land; some did it necessarily, and some for their owne pleasure, but it brought to the most, if not to all, coughes and colds, the weather prouing sodainly cold and stormie, which afterward turned to the scurvey, whereof many dyed.

When

When our Shallop was fit indeed, before she was fully fitted, for there was two dayes worke after bestowed on her, there was appointed some 24 men of our owne, and armed, then to goe and make a more full discovery of the rivers before mentioned. Master *Iones* was desirous to goe with vs, and tooke such of his saylers as he thought vsefull for vs, so as we were in all about 34. men; wee made master *Iones* our Leader, for we thought it best herein to gratifie his kindnes and forwardnes. When we were set forth, it proued rough weather and crosse windes, so as we were constrained, some in the Shallop, and others in the long Boate, to row to the neerest shore the wind would suffer them to goe vnto, and then to wade out aboue the knees; the wind was so strong as the Shallop could not keepe the water, but was forced to harbour there that night, but we marched sixe or seauen miles further, and appointed the Shallop to come to vs as soone as they could. It blowed and did snow all that day & night, and frose withall; some of our people that are dead tooke the originall of their death here. The next day about 11. a clocke our Shallop came to vs, and wee shipped our selues, and the wind being good, we sayled to the river we formerly discovered, which we named, *Cold Harbour*, to which when wee came we found it not Navigable for Ships, yet we thought it might be a good harbour for Boats, for it flowes there 12. foote at high water. We landed our men betweene the two creekes, and marched some foure or fiue myles by the greater of them, and the Shallop followed vs; at length night grew on, and our men were tired with marching vp and downe the steepe hills, and deepe vallies, which lay halfe a foot thicke with snow: Master *Iones* wearied with marching, was desirous we should take vp our lodging, though some of vs would haue marched further; so we made there our Randevous for that night, vnder a few Pine trees, and as it fell out, wee got three fat Geese, and six Ducks to our Supper, which we eate with Souldiers stomacks, for we had eaten little all that day; our resolution was next morning to goe vp to the head of this river, for we supposed it would proue fresh water, but in the morning our refolution held not, becaufe many liked not the hillineffe of the foyle, and badneffe of the harbour, fo we turned towards the other creeke, that wee might goe over and looke for the reft of the Corne that we left behind when we were here before; when we came to the creeke, we faw the Canow lie on the dry ground, and a flocke of Geefe in the river, at which one made a fhot, and killed a couple of them, and we lanched the Canow & fetcht them, and when we had done, fhe carryed vs over by feaven or eight at once. This done, we marched to the place where we had the corne formerly, which place we called *Corne-hyll*; and digged and found the reft, of which we were very glad: we alfo digged in a place a little further off, and found a Botle of oyle; wee went to another place, which we had feene before, and digged, and found more corne, *viz.* two or three Baskets full of *Indian* Wheat, and a bag of Beanes, with a good many of faire Wheat-eares; whilft fome of vs were digging vp this, fome others found another heape of Corne, which they digged vp alfo, fo as we had in all about ten Bufhels, which will ferue vs fufficiently for feed. And fure it was Gods good providence that we found this Corne, for els wee know not how we fhould haue done, for we knew not how we fhould find, or meete with any of the *Indians*, except it be to doe vs a mifchiefe. Alfo we had neuer in all likelihood feene a graine of it, if we had not made our firft Iourney; for the ground was now covered with fnow, and fo hard frofen, that we were faine with our Curtlaxes and fhort Swords, to hew and carue the ground a foot deepe, and then wreft it vp with leavers, for we had forgot to bring other Tooles; whilft we were in this imployment, foule weather being towards, Mafter *Iones* was earneft to goe abourd, but fundry of vs defired to make further difcovery, and to find out the *Indians* habitations, fo we fent home with him our weakeft people, and fome that were ficke, and all the Corne, and 18. of vs ftayed ftill, and lodged there that night, and defired that the Shallop might returne to vs next day, and bring vs fome Mattocks and Spades with them.

The

Note.

The next morning we followed certaine beaten pathes and tracts of the *Indians* into the Woods, suppoſing they would haue led vs into ſome Towne, or houſes; after wee had gone a while, we light, vpon a very broad beaten path, well nigh two foote broad, then we lighted all our Matches, and prepared our ſelues, concluding wee were neare their dwellings, but in the end we found it to be onely a path made to driue Deere in, when the *Indians* hunt, as wee ſuppoſed; when we had marched fiue or ſix myles into the Woods, and could find no ſignes of any people, we returned againe another way, and as we came into the plaine ground, wee found a place like a graue, but it was much bigger and longer then any we had yet ſeene. It was alſo covered with boords, ſo as we muſed what it ſhould be, and reſolved to digge it vp, where we found, firſt a Matt, and vnder that a fayre Bow, and there another Matt, and vnder that a boord about three quarters long, finely carued and paynted, with three tynes, or broches on the top, like a Crowne; alſo betweene the Matts we found Boules, Trayes, Diſhes, and ſuch like Trinkets; at length we came to a faire new Matt, and vnder that two Bundles, the one bigger, the other leſſe, we opened the greater and found in it a great quantitie of fine and perfect red Powder, and in it the bones and skull of a man. The skull had fine yellow haire ſtill on it, and ſome of the fleſh vnconſumed; there was bound vp with it a knife, a pack-needle, and two or three old iron things. It was bound vp in a Saylers canvas Caſacke, and a payre of cloth breeches; the red Powder was a kind of Embaulment, and yeelded a ſtrong, but no offenſiue ſmell; It was as fine as any flower. We opened the leſſe bundle likewiſe, and found of the ſame Powder in it, and the bones and head of a little childe, about the leggs, and other parts of it was bound ſtrings, and bracelets of fine white Beads; there was alſo by it a little Bow, about three quarters long. and ſome other odd knackes; we brought ſundry of the pretieſt things away with vs, and covered the Corps vp againe. After this, we digged in ſundry like places, but found no more Corne, nor any things els but

graues:

graues: There was varietie of opinions amongst vs about the embalmed perſon ; ſome thought it was an *Indian* Lord and King : others ſayd, the *Indians* haue all blacke hayre, and never any was ſeene with browne or yellow hayre ; ſome thought, it was a Chriſtian of ſome ſpeciall note, which had dyed amongſt them, and they thus buried him to honour him ; others thought, they had killed him, and did it in triumph over him. Whileſt we were thus ranging and ſearching, two of the Saylers, which were newly come on the ſhore, by chance eſpied two houſes, which had beene lately dwelt in, but the people were gone. They having their peeces, and hearing no body entred the houſes, and tooke out ſome things, and durſt not ſtay but came againe and told vs ; ſo ſome ſeauen or eight of vs went with them, and found how we had gone within a flight ſhot of them before. The houſes were made with long yong Sapling trees, bended and both ends ſtucke into the ground ; they were made round, like vnto an Arbour, and covered downe to the ground with thicke and well wrought matts, and the doore was not over a yard high, made of a matt to open ; the chimney was a wide open hole in the top, for which they had a matt to cover it cloſe when they pleaſed ; one might ſtand and goe vpright in them, in the midſt of them were foure little trunches knockt into the ground, and ſmall ſtickes laid over, on which they hung their Pots, and what they had to ſeeth ; round about the fire they lay on matts, which are their beds. The houſes were double matted, for as they were matted without, ſo were they within, with newer & fairer matts. In the houſes we found wooden Boules, Trayes & Diſhes, Earthen Pots, Hand baskets made of Crab ſhells, wrought together ; alſo an Engliſh Paile or Bucket, it wanted a bayle, but it had two Iron eares : there was alſo Baskets of ſundry ſorts, bigger and ſome leſſer, finer and ſome courſer : ſome were curiouſly wrought with blacke and white in pretie workes, and ſundry other of their houſhold ſtuffe: we found alſo two or three Deeres heads, one whereof had bin newly killed, for it was ſtill freſh ; there was alſo a company of

Deeres

Deeres feete, stuck vp in the houses, Harts hornes, and Eagles clawes, and sundry such like things there was : also two or three Baskets full of parched Acornes, peeces of fish, and a peece of a broyled Hering. We found also a little silke grasse, and a little Tobacco seed, with some other seeds which wee knew not ; without was sundry bundles of Flags, and Sedge, Bull rushes, and other stuffe to make matts ; there was thrust into an hollow tree, two or three peeces of Venison, but we thought it fitter for the Dogs then for vs : some of the best things we tooke away with vs, and left the houses standing still as they were, so it growing towards night, and the tyde almost spent, we hasted with our things downe to the Shallop, and got abourd that night, intending to haue brought some Beades, and other things to haue left in the houses, in signe of Peace, and that we meant to truk with them, but it was not done, by meanes of our hastie comming away from Cape Cod, but so soone as we can meete conveniently with them, we will giue them full satisfaction. Thus much of our second Discovery.

Having thus discovered this place, it was controversall amongst vs, what to doe touching our aboad and setling there ; some thought it best for many reasons to abide there.

As first, that there was a convenient harbour for Boates, though not for Ships.

Secondly, Good Corne ground readie to our hands, as we saw by experience in the goodly corne it yeelded, which would againe agree with the ground, and be naturall seed for the same.

Thirdly, Cape Cod was like to be a place of good fishing, for we saw daily great Whales of the best kind for oyle and bone, come close abourd our Ship, and in fayre weather swim and play about vs ; there was once one when the Sun shone warme, came and lay aboue water, as if she had beene dead, for a good while together, within halfe a Musket shot of the Ship, at which two were prepared to shoote, to see whether she would stir or no, he that gaue fire first, his Musket flew in peeces, both stocke and barrell, yet thankes be to

D 3 God

God, neither he nor any man els was hurt with it, though
many were there about, but when the Whale faw her time
fhe gaue a fnuffe and away.

Fourthly, the place was likely to be healthfull, fecure, and
defenfible.

But the laft and efpeciall reafon was, that now the heart of
Winter and vnfeafonable weather was come vpon vs, fo
that we could not goe vpon coafting and difcovery, without danger of loofing men and Boat, vpon which would
follow the overthrow of all, efpecially confidering what va-
riable windes and fodaine ftormes doe there arife. Alfo cold
and wett lodging had fo taynted our people, for fcarce any
of vs were free from vehement coughs, as if they fhould continue long in that eftate, it would indanger the liues of many, and breed difeafes and infection amongft vs. Againe,
we had yet fome Beere, Butter, Flefh, and other fuch victuals left, which would quickly be all gone, and then we fhould
haue nothing to comfort vs in the great labour and toyle we
were like to vnder-goe at the firft ; It was alfo conceived,
whilft we had competent victuals, that the Ship would ftay
with vs, but when that grew low, they would be gone, and
let vs fhift as we could.

Others againe, vrged greatly the going to *Anguum* or
Angoum, a place twentie leagues off to the North-wards,
which they had heard to be an excellent harbour for fhips ;
better ground and better fifhing. Secondly for any thing we
knew, there might be hard by vs a farre better feate, and it
fhould be a great hindrance to feate where wee fhould remoue againe. Thirdly, The water was but in ponds, and it
was thought there would be none in Summer, or very little. Fourthly, the water there muft be fetched vp a fteepe
hill: but to omit many reafons and replies vfed heere a-
bouts ; It was in the ende concluded, to make fome difcovery within the Bay, but in no cafe fo farre as *Angoum* : befides, *Robert Coppin* our Pilot, made relation of a great Navigable River and good harbour in the other head-land of
this Bay, almoft right over againft *Cape Cod*, being a right
line,

line, not much aboue eight leagues diftant, in which hee had beene once: and becaufe that one of the wild men with whom they had fome trucking, ftole a harping Iron from them, they called it theeuifh harbour. And beyond that place they were cnioyned not to goe, whereupon, a Company was chofen to goe out vppon a third difcovery : whileft fome were imployed in this difcovery, it pleafed God that Miftris *White* was brought a bed of a Sonne, which was called *Peregrine*.

The fift day, we through Gods mercy efcaped a great danger by the foolifhnes of a Boy, one of *Francis Billingtons* Sonnes, who in his Fathers abfence, had got Gun-powder, and had fhot of a peice or two, and made fquibs, and there being a fowling peice charged in his fathers Cabbin, fhot her off in the Cabbin, there being a little barrell of powder halfe full, fcattered in and about the Cabbin, the fire being within foure foote of the bed betweene the Deckes, and many flints and Iron things about the Cabbin, and many people about the fire, and yet by Gods mercy no harme done.

Wednefday the fixt of December, it was refolved our difcoverers fhould fet forth, for the day before was too fowle weather, and fo they did, though it was well ore the day ere all things could be readie: So ten of our men were appointed who were of themfelues willing to vndertake it, to wit, Captaine *Standifh*, Maifter *Carver*, *William Bradford*, *Edward Winfloe*, *Iohn Tilley*, *Edward Tilley*, *Iohn Houland*, and three of London, *Richard Warren*, *Steeuen Hopkins* and *Edward Dotte*, and two of our Sea-men, *Iohn Alderton* and *Thomas Englifh*, of the Ships Company there went two of the Mafters Mates, Mafter *Clarke* and Mafter *Copin*, the Mafter Gunner, and three Saylers. The narration of which Difcovery, followes, penned by one of the Company.

Wednefday the fixt of December wee fet out, being very cold and hard weather, wee were a long while after we launched from the fhip, before we could get cleare of a fandie poynt, which lay within leffe then a furlong of the fame. In which time, two were very ficke, and *Edward Tilley* had like

to

to haue sounded with cold ; the Gunner was also sicke vnto
Death, (but hope of truking made him to goe) and so remained all that day, and the next night ; at length we got cleare
of the sandy poynt, and got vp our sayles, and within an
houre or two we got vnder the weather shore, and then had
smoother water and better sayling, but it was very cold, for,
the water frose on our clothes, and made them many times
like coats of Iron : wee sayled fixe or seauen leagues by the
shore, but saw neither river nor creeke, at length wee mett
with a tongue of Land, being flat off from the shore, with a
sandy poynt, we bore vp to gaine the poynt, & found there
a fayre income or rode, of a Bay, being a league over at the
narrowest, and some two or three in length, but wee made
right over to the land before vs, and left the discovery of this
Income till the next day : as we drew neare to the shore, wee
espied some ten or twelue *Indians*, very busie about a blacke
thing, what it was we could not tell, till afterwards they saw
vs, and ran to and fro, as if they had beene carrying some
thing away, wee landed a league or two from them, and had
much adoe to put a shore any where, it lay so full of flat sands,
when we came to shore, we made vs a Baricado, and got fire
wood, and set out our Sentinells, and betooke vs to our lodging, such as it was ; we saw the smoke of the fire which the
Savages made that night, about foure or fiue myles from vs,
in the morning we devided our company, some eight in the
Shallop, and the rest on the shore went to discouer this place,
but we found it onely to be a Bay, without either river or
creeke comming into it, yet we deemed it to be as good an
harbour as Cape Cod, for they that sounded it, found a ship
might ride in fiue fathom water, wee on the land found it to
be a levill soyle, but none of the fruitfullest ; wee saw two
beckes of fresh water, which were the first running streames
that we saw in the Country, but one might stride over them :
we found also a great fish, called a *Grampus* dead on the sands,
they in the Shallop found two of them also in the bottome
of the bay, dead in like sort, they were cast vp at high water,
and could not get off for the frost and ice ; they were some
                                                          fiue

fiue or fixe paces long, and about two inches thicke of fat, and flefhed like a Swine, they would haue yeelded a great deale of oyle, if there had beene time and meanes to haue taken it, fo we finding nothing for our turne, both we and our Shallop returned. We then directed our courfe along the Sea-fands, to the place where we firft faw the *Indians*, when we were there, we faw it was alfo a *Grampus* which they were cutting vp, they cut it into long rands or peeces, about an ell long, and two handfull broad, wee found here and there a peece fcattered by the way, as it feemed, for hast: this place the moft were minded we fhould call, the *Grampus Bay*, becaufe we found fo many of them there : wee followed the tract of the *Indians* bare feete a good way on the fands, at length we faw where they ftrucke into the Woods by the fide of a Pond, as wee went to view the place, one layd, hee thought hee faw an *Indian*-houfe among the trees, fo went vp to fee: and here we and the Shallop loft fight one of another till night, it being now about nine or ten a clocke, fo we light on a path, but faw no houfe, and followed a great way into the woods, at length wee found where Corne had beene fet, but not that yeare, anone we found a great burying place, one part whereof was incompaffed with a large Palazado, like a Church-yard, with yong fpires foure or fiue yards long, fet as clofe one by another as they could two or three foot in the ground, within it was full of Graues, fome bigger, and fome leffe, fome were alfo paled about, & others had like an *Indian*-houfe made over them, but not matted : thofe Graues were more fumptuous then thofe at *Corne-hill*, yet we digged none of them vp, but onely viewed them, and went our way ; without the Palazado were graues alfo, but not fo coftly : from this place we went and found more Corne ground, but not of this yeare. As we ranged we light on foure or fiue *Indian*-houfes, which had beene lately dwelt in, but they were vncovered, and had no matts about them, els they were like thofe we found at *Corne-hill*, but had not beehe fo lately dwelt in, there was nothing left but two or three peeces of old matts, a little fedge, alfo a little further we

E   found

found two Baskets full of parched Acorns hid in the ground, which we supposed had beene Corne when we beganne to dig the same, we cast earth thereon againe & went our way. All this while we saw no people, wee went ranging vp and downe till the Sunne began to draw low, and then we hasted out of the woods, that we might come to our Shallop, which when we were out of the woods, we espied a great way off, and call'd them to come vnto vs, the which they did as soone as they could, for it was not yet high water, they were exceeding glad to see vs, (for they feared because they had not seene vs in so long a time) thinking we would haue kept by the shore side, so being both weary and faint, for we had eaten nothing all that day, we fell to make our Randevous and get fire wood, which alwayes cost vs a great deale of labour, by that time we had done, & our Shallop come to vs, it was within night, and we fed vpon such victualls as we had, and betooke vs to our rest, after we had set out our watch. About midnight we heard a great and hideous cry, and our Sentinell called, *Arme, Arme.* So we bestirred our selues and shot off a couple of Muskets, and noyse ceased; we concluded, that it was a company of Wolues or Foxes, for one told vs, hee had heard such a noyse in *New-found land.* About fiue a clocke in the morning wee began to be stirring, and two or three which doubted whether their Peeces would goe off or no made tryall of them, and shot them off, but thought nothing at all, after Prayer we prepared our selues for brek-fast, and for a journey, and it being now the twilight in the morning, it was thought meet to carry the things downe to the Shallop : some sayd, it was not best to carry the Armour downe, others sayd, they would be readier, two or three sayd, they would not carry theirs, till they went themselues, but mistrusting nothing at all : as it fell out, the water not being high enough, they layd the things downe vpon the shore, & came vp to brek-fast. Anone, all vpon a sudden, we heard a great & strange cry, which we knew to be the same voyces, though they varied their notes, one of our company being abroad came running in, and cryed, *They are men, Indians, Indians ;*

and

and withall, their arrowes came flying amongſt vs, our men
ran out with all ſpeed to recover their armes, as by the good
Providence of God they did. In the meane time, Captaine Our firſt com-
Miles Standiſh, having a ſnaphance ready, made a ſhot, and bat with the
after him another, after they two had ſhot, other two of vs *Indians.*
were ready, but he wiſht vs not to ſhoot, till we could take
ayme, for we knew not what need we ſhould haue, & there
were foure onely of vs, which had their armes there readie,
and ſtood before the open ſide of our Baricado, which was
firſt aſſaulted, they thought it beſt to defend it, leaſt the ene-
mie ſhould take it and our ſtuffe, and ſo haue the more van-
tage againſt vs, our care was no leſſe for the Shallop, but we
hoped all the reſt would defend it; we called vnto them to
know how it was with them, and they anſwered, Well, Well
every one, and be of good courage: wee heard three of their
Peeces goe off, and the reſt called for a fire-brand to light
their matches, one tooke a log out of the fire on his ſhoulder
and went and carried it vnto them, which was thought did
not a little diſcourage our enemies. The cry of our enemies
was dreadfull, eſpecially, when our men ran out to recover
their Armes, their note was after this manner, *Woath woach
ha ha hach woach* : our men were no ſooner come to their
Armes, but the enemy was ready to aſſault them.

There was a luſtie man and no whit leſſe valiant, who was
thought to bee their Captaine, ſtood behind a tree within
halfe a musket ſhot of vs, and there let his arrowes fly at vs ;
hee was ſeene to ſhoote three arrowes, which were all avoyded, for he at whom the firſt arrow was aymed, ſaw it, and
ſtooped downe and it flew over him , the reſt were avoyded
alſo : he ſtood three ſhots of a Musket, at length one tooke
as he ſayd full ayme at him, after which he gaue an extraordinary cry and away they went all , wee followed them a-
bout a quarter of a mile, but wee left ſixe to keepe our Shallop, for we were carefull of our buſineſſe : then wee ſhouted
all together two ſeverall times, and ſhot off a couple of muskets and ſo returned : this wee did that they might ſee wee
were not afrayd of them nor diſcouraged. Thus it pleaſed

God

God to vanquifh our Enemies and giue vs deliuerance, by
their noyfe we could not gueffe that they were leffe then thirty or forty, though fome thought that they were many more
yet in the darke of the morning, wee could not fo well dif-
cerne them among the trees, as they could feevs by our fire
fide, we tooke vp 18. of their arrowes which we haue fent
to *England* by Mafter *Iones*, fome whereof were headed with
Braffe, others with Harts horne, & others with Eagles clawes
many more no doubt were fhot, for thefe we found, were
almoft couered with leaues: yet by the efpeciall providence
of God, none of them either hit or hurt vs, though many
came clofe by vs, and on every fide of vs, and fome coates
which hung vp in our Baricado, were fhot through and
through. So after wee had given God thankes for our deli-
verance, wee tooke our Shallop and went on our Iourney,
and called this place, *The firft Encounter*, from hence we intended to haue fayled to the aforefayd theeuifh Harbour, if
wee found no convenient Harbour by the way, having the
wind good, we fayled all that day along the Coaft about 15.
leagues, but faw neither River nor Creeke to put into, after we had fayled an houre or two, it began to fnow and
raine, and to be bad weather; about the midft of the after-
noone, the winde increafed and the Seas began to be very
rough, and the hinges of the rudder broke, fo that we could
fteere no longer with it, but two men with much adoe were
faine to ferue with a couple of Oares, the Seas were growne
fo great, that we were much troubled and in great daunger,
and night grew on: Anon Mafter *Coppin* bad vs be of good
cheere he faw the Harbour, as we drew neare, the gale being ftiffe, and we bearing great fayle to get in, fplit our Maft
in 3. peices, and were like to haue caft away our Shallop, yet
by Gods mercy recovering our felues, wee had the floud
with vs, and ftruck into the Harbour.

Now he that thought that had beene the place was deceived, it being a place where not any of vs had beene before,
and comming into the Harbour, he that was our Pilot did
beare vp North-ward, which if we had continued wee had
beene

beene caſt away, yet ſtill the Lord kept vs, and we bare vp
for an Iland before vs, and recovering of that Iland, being
compaſſed about with many Rocks, and darke night growing vpon vs, it pleaſed the Divine providence that we fell
vpon a place of ſandy ground, where our Shallop did ride
ſafe and ſecure all that night, and comming vpon a ſtrange
Iland kept our watch all night in the raine vpon that Iland :
and in the morning we marched about it, & found no Inhabitants at all, and here wee made our Randevous all that day,
being Saturday, 10. of December, on the Sabboth day wee
reſted, and on Munday we ſounded the Harbour, and found
it a very good Harbour for our ſhipping, we marched alſo
into the Land, and found divers corne fields, and little running brookes, a place very good for ſcituation, ſo we returned to our Ship againe with good newes to the reſt of our
people, which did much comfort their hearts.

On the fifteenth day, we waighed Anchor, to goe to the
place we had diſcovered, and comming within two leagues
of the Land, we could not fetch the Harbour, but were faine
to put roome againe towards *Cape Cod*, our courſe lying
Weſt; and the wind was at North weſt, but it pleaſed God
that the next day being Saturday the 16. day, the winde came
faire, and wee put to Sea againe, and came ſafely into a ſafe
Harbour ; and within halfe an houre the winde changed, ſo
as if we had beene letted but a little, we had gone backe to
Cape Cod. This Harbour is a Bay greater then *Cape Cod*,
compaſſed with a goodly Land, and in the Bay, 2. fine Ilands
vninhabited, wherein are nothing but wood, Okes, Pines,
Wal-nut, Beech, Saſifras, Vines, and other trees which wee
know not ; This Bay is a moſt hopefull place, innumerable
ſtore of fowle, and excellent good, and cannot but bee of
fiſh in their ſeaſons : Skote, Cod, Turbot, and Herring, wee
haue taſted of, abundance of Muſſes the greateſt & beſt that
ever we ſaw ; Crabs, and Lobſters, in their time infinite, It
is in faſhion like a Cikle or Fiſh-hooke.

Munday the 13. day, we went a land, manned with the
Maiſter of the Ship, and 3. or 4. of the Saylers, we marched

along

along the coaſt in the woods, ſome 7. or 8. mile, but ſaw not an *Indian* nor an *Indian* houſe, only we found where former-ly, had beene ſome Inhabitants, and where they had planted their corne: we found not any Navigable River, but 4. or 5. ſmall running brookes of very ſweet freſh water, that all run into the Sea : The Land for the cruſt of the earth is a ſpits depth, excellent blacke mold and fat in ſome places, 2. or 3. great Oakes but not very thicke, Pines, Wal-nuts Beech Aſh, Birch, Haſell, Holley, Aſp, Saſifras, in abundance, & Vines every where, Cherry trees, Plum trees, and many other which we know not; many kinds of hearbes, we found heere in Winter, as Strawbery leaues innumerable, Sorrell, Yarow, Caruell, Brook-lime, Liver-wort, Water-creſſes, great ſtore of Leekes, and Onyons, and an excellent ſtrong kind of Flaxe, and Hempe; here is ſand, gravell, and excel-lent clay no better in the Worlde, excellent for pots, and will waſh like ſope, and great ſtore of ſtone, though ſome-what ſoft, and the beſt water that ever we drunke, and the Brookes now begin to be full of fiſh; that night many being weary with marching, wee went abourd againe.

The next morning being Tueſday the 19. of December, wee went againe to diſcover further; ſome went on Land, and ſome in the Shallop, the Land we found as the former day we did, and we found a Creeke, and went vp three En-gliſh myles, a very pleaſant river at full Sea, a Barke of thirty tunne may goe vp, but at low water ſcarce our Shallop could paſſe : this place we had a great liking to plant in, but that it was ſo farre from our fiſhing our principall profit, and ſo incompaſſed with woods, that we ſhould bee in much dan-ger of the Salvages, and our number being ſo little, and ſo much ground to cleare, ſo as wee thought good to quit and cleare that place, till we were of more ſtrength; ſome of vs hauing a good minde for ſafety to plant in the greater Ile, wee croſſed the Bay which there is fiue or ſixe myles ouer, and found the Ile about a myle and a halfe, or two myles a-bout, all wooded, and no freſh water but 2. or 3. pits, that we doubted of freſh water in Summer, and ſo full of wood, as we could hardly cleare so much as to serue vs for Corne, besides wee iudged it colde for our Corne, and some part very rockie, yet diuers thought of it as a place defensible, and of great securitie.

That night we returned againe a ship boord, with resolution the next morning to setle on some of those places, so in the morning, after we had called on God for direction, we came to this resolution, to goe presently ashore againe, and to take a better view of two places, which wee thought most fittting for vs, for we could not now take time for further search or consideration, our victuals being much spent, especially, our Beere, and it being now the 19. of *December*. After our landing and viewing of the places, so well as we could we came to a conclusion, by most voyces, to set on the maine Land, on the first place, on an high ground, where there is a great deale of Land cleared, and hath beene planted with Corne three or foure yeares agoe, and there is a very sweet brooke runnes vnder the hill side, and many delicate springs of as good water as can be drunke, and where we may harbour o.. ... llops and Boates exceeding well, and in this broo.. ... good fish in their seasons: on the further side of the ... mo much Corne ground cleared, in one field is a great hill, on which wee poynt to make a plat-forme, and plant our Ordinance, which will command all round about, from thence we may see into the *Bay*, and farre into the Sea, and we may see thence *Cape Cod*: our greatest labour will be fetching of our wood, which is halfe a quarter of an English myle, but there is enough so farre off; what people inhabite here we yet know not, for as yet we haue seene none, so there we made our Randevous, and a place for some of our people about twentie, resolving in the morning to come all ashore, and to build houses, but the next morning being Thursday the 21. of *December*, it was stormie and wett, that we could not goe ashore, and those that remained there all night could doe nothing, but were wet, not having dai-light enough to make them a sufficient court of gard, to keepe them dry. All that night it blew and rayned extreamely;

it

it was so tempestuous, that the Shallop could not goe on land so soone as was meet, for they had no victuals on land. About 11. a Clocke the Shallop went off with much adoe with provision, but could not returne it blew so strong, and was such foule weather, that we were forced to let fall our Anchor, and ride with three Anchors an head.

Friday the 22. the storme still continued, that we could not get a-land, nor they come to vs aboord: this morning Good wife *Alderton* was delivered of a sonne, but dead borne.

Saturday the 23. so many of vs as could, went on shore, felled and carried tymber, to provide themselues stuffe for building.

Sunday the 24. our people on shore heard a cry of some Savages (as they thought) which caused an Alarm, and to stand on their gard. expecting an assault, but all was quiet.

Munday the 25. day, we went on shore, some to fell tymber, some to saw, some to riue, and some to carry, so no man rested all that day, but towards night some as they were at worke, heard a noyse of some *Indians*, which   vs all to goe to our Muskets, but we heard no furth   came aboord againe, and left some twentie to keepe the court of gard ; that night we had a sore storme of winde and rayne.

Munday the 25. being Christmas day, we began to drinke water aboord, but at night the Master caused vs to haue some Beere, and so on boord we had diverse times now and then some Beere, but on shore none at all.

Tuesday the 26. it was foule weather, that we could not goe ashore.

Wednesday the 27. we went to worke againe.

Thursday the 28. of *December*, so many as could went to worke on the hill, where we purposed to build our platforme for our Ordinance, and which doth command all the plaine, and the *Bay*, and from whence we may see farre into the sea, and might be easier impayled, having two rowes of houses and a faire streete. So in the afternoone we went to measure out the grounds, and first, we tooke notice how many Fami-

Families they were, willing all single men that had no wives to ioyne with some Familie, as they thought fit, that so we might build fewer houses, which was done, and we reduced them to 19.Families ; to greater Families we allotted larger plots, to every person halfe a pole in breadth, and three in length, and so Lots were cast where euery man should lie, which was done, and staked out ; we thought this proportion was large enough at the first, for houses and gardens, to impale them round, considering the weaknes of our people, many of them growing ill with coldes, for our former Discoveries in frost and stormes, and the wading at Cape *Cod* had brought much weakenes amongst vs, which increased so every day more and more, and after was the cause of many of their deaths.

Fryday and Saturday, we fitted our selues for our labour, but our people on shore were much troubled and discouraged with rayne and wett that day, being very stormie and cold ; we saw great smokes of fire made by the *Indians* about six or seauen myles from vs as we coniectured.

Munday the first of *Ianuary*, we went betimes to worke, we were much hindred in lying so farre off from the Land, and faine to goe as the tyde serued, that we lost much time, for our Ship drew so much water, that she lay a myle and almost a halfe off, though a ship of seauentie or eightie tun at high water may come to the shore.

Wednesday the third of *Ianuary*, some of our people being abroad, to get and gather thatch, they saw great fires of the *Indians*, and were at their Corne fields, yet saw none of the Savages, nor had seene any of them since wee came to this Bay.

Thursday the fourth of *Ianuary*, Captaine *Miles Standish* with foure or fiue more, went to see if they could meet with any of the Savages in that place where the fires were made, they went to some of their houses, but not lately inhabited, yet could they not meete with any ; as they came home, they shot at an Eagle and killed her, which was excellent meat ; It was hardly to be discerned from Mutton.

F   Fryday

Fryday the fifth of *Ianuary*, one of the Saylers found aliue vpon the ſhore an Hering, which the Maſter had to his ſupper, which put vs in hope of fiſh, but as yet we had got but one Cod ; we wanted ſmall hookes.

Saturday the ſixt of *Ianuary*, Maſter *Marten* was very ſicke, and to our iudgement, no hope of life, ſo Maſter *Carver* was ſent for to come abourd to ſpeake with him about his accompts, who came the next morning.

Munday the eight day of *Ianuary*, was a very fayre day, and we went betimes to worke, maſter *Iones* ſent the Shallop as he had formerly done, to ſee where fiſh could be got, they had a great ſtorme at Sea, and were in ſome danger, at night they returned with three great Seales, and an excellent good Cod, which did aſſure vs that we ſhould haue plentie of fiſh ſhortly.

This day, *Francis Billington*, having the weeke before ſeene from the top of a tree on an hie hill, a great ſea as he thought, went with one of the Maſters mates to ſee it, they went three myles, and then came to a great water, devided into two great Lakes, the bigger of them fiue or ſixe myles in circuit, and in it an Ile of a Cable length ſquare, the other three miles in compaſſe ; in their eſtimation they are fine freſh water, full of fiſh, and foule ; a brooke iſſues from it, it will be an excellent helpe for vs in time. They found ſeaven or eight *Indian* houſes, but not lately inhabited, when they ſaw the houſes they were in ſome feare, for they were but two perſons and one peece.

Tueſday the 9. Ianuary, was a reaſonable faire day, and wee went to labour that day in the building of our Towne, in two rowes of houſes for more ſafety : we devided by lott the plot of ground whereon to build our Towne : After the proportion formerly allotted, wee agreed that every man ſhould build his owne houſe, thinking by that courſe, men would make more haſt then working in common : the common houſe, in which for the firſt, we made our Rendevous, being neere finiſhed wanted onely couering, it being about 20. foote ſquare, ſome ſhould make morter, and ſome

some gather thatch, so that in foure dayes halfe of it was that-
ched, frost and foule weather hindred vs much, this time
of the yeare seldome could wee worke halfe the wecke.

Thursday the eleuenth, *William Bradford* being at worke,
(for it was a faire day) was vehemently taken with a griefe
and paine, and so shot to his huckle-bone ; It was doubted
that he would haue instantly dyed, hee got colde in the former discoueries, especially the last, and felt some paine in
his anckles by times, but he grew a little better towards night
and in time through Gods mercie in the vse of meanes reco-
vered.

Friday the 12. we went to worke, but about noone, it
began to raine, that it forced vs to giue over worke.

This day, two of our people put vs in great sorrow and
care, there was 4. sent to gather and cut thatch in the morning, and two of them, *Iohn Goodman* and *Peter Browne*,
having cut thatch all the fore noone, went to a further place,
and willed the other two, to binde vp that which was cut
and to follow them ; so they did, being about a myle and
an halfe from our Plantation : but when the two came after, they could not finde them, nor heare any thing of them
at all, though they hallowed and shouted as loud as they
could, so they returned to the Company and told them of
it: whereupon Master *Leaver* & three or foure more went to
seeke them , but could heare nothing of them, so they retur-
ning, sent more, but that night they could heare nothing at
all of them: the next day they armed 10. or 12. men out,
verily thinking the *Indians* had surprised them , they went
seeking 7. or 8. myles, but could neither see nor heare any
thing at all, so they returned with much discomfort to vs
all. These two that were missed, at dinner time tooke
their meate in their hands, and would goe walke and refresh themselues, so going a litle off they finde a lake of water, and having a great Mastiffe bitch with them and a Spannell ; by the water side they found a great Deere, the Dogs
chased him , and they followed so farre as they lost themselues, and could not finde the way backe , they wandred

all that after-noone being wett, and at night it did freeze
and snow, they were slenderly apparelled and had no wea-
pons but each one his Cicle, nor any victuals , they ranged
vp and downe and could finde none of the Salvages habitations ; when it drew to night they were much perplexed,
for they could finde neither harbour nor meate, but in frost
and snow, were forced to make the earth their bed, and the
Element their covering , and another thing did very much
terrifie them, they heard as they thought two Lyons roaring
exceedingly for a long time together, and a third, that they
thought was very nere them, so not knowing what to do, they
resolved to climbe vp into a tree as their safest refuge, though
that would proue an intollerable colde lodging ; so they
stoode at the trees roote , that when the Lyons came they
might take their opportunitie of climbing vp, the bitch they
were faine to hold by the necke, for shee would haue beene
gone to the Lyon ; but it pleased God so to dispose, that the
wilde Beastes came not : so they walked vp and downe vnder the Tree all night , it was an extreame colde night , so
soone as it was light they trauailed againe, passing by many
lakes and brookes and woods , and in one place where the
Salvages had burnt the space of 5. myles in length , which
is a fine Champion Countrey, and even. In the after-noone,
it pleased God from an high Hill they discovered the two
Iles in the Bay, and so that night got to the Plantation, being ready to faint with travaile and want of victuals , and
almost famished with colde, *Iohn Goodmen* was faine to haue
his shooes cut off his feete they were so swelled with colde,
and it was a long while after ere he was able to goe ; those
on the shore were much comforted at their returne, but they
on ship-boord were grieved as deeming them lost ; but the
next day being the 14. of Ianuary, in the morning about
sixe of the clocke the winde being very great, they on ship-
boord spied their great new Randevous on fire, which was
to them a new discomfort, fearing because of the supposed
losse of the men. that the Salvages had fiered them, neither
could they presently goe to them for want of water, but after

ter 3. quarters of an houre they went , as they had purposed
the day before to keepe the Sabboth on shore , because now
there was the greater number of people. At their landing
they heard good tidings of the returne of the 2. men, and
that the house was fiered occasionally by a sparke that flew
into the thatch, which instantly burnt it all vp, but the roofe
stood and little hurt ; the most losse was Maister *Carvers* and
William Bradfords, who then lay sicke in bed, and if they had
not risen with good speede, had beene blowne vp with powder : but through Gods mercy they had no harme, the house
was as full of beds as they could lie one by another, and their
Muskets charged, but blessed be God there was no harme
done.

Munday the 15. day, it rayned much all day, that they on
ship-boord could not goe on shore, nor they on shore doe a-
ny labour but were all wet.

Tuesday, wednesday, thursday, were very faire Sun-shinie
dayes, as if it had beene in Aprill, and our people so many as
were in health wrought chearefully.

The 19 day, we resolved to make a Shed, to put our common provision in, of which some were alreadie set on shore,
but at noone it rayned, that we could not worke. This day
in the evening, *Iohn Goodman* went abroad to vse his lame
feete, that were pittifully ill with the cold he had got, having
a little Spannell with him, a little way from the Plantation,
two great Wolues ran after the Dog, the Dog ran to him
and betwixt his leggs for succour, he had nothing in his hand
but tooke vp a sticke, and threw at one of them and hit him,
and they presently ran both away, but came againe, he got a
paile bord in his hand, and they sat both on their tayles,
grinning at him, a good while, and went their way, and left
him.

Saturday 20. we made vp our Shed for our commongoods.

Sunday the 21. we kept our meeting on Land.

Munday the 22. was a faire day, we wrought on our houses, and in the after-noone carried vp our hogsheads of meale
to our common store house.

F 3   The

The reſt of the weeke we followed our buſineſſe likewiſe.

Munday the 29. in the morning cold froſt and ſleete, but after reaſonable fayre ; both the long Boate and the Shallop brought our common goods on ſhore.

Tueſday and wedneſday 30. and 31. of *Ianuary*, cold froſty weather and ſleete, that we could not worke: in the morning the Maſter and others ſaw two Savages, that had beene on the Iland nere our Ship, what they came for wee could not tell, they were going ſo farre backe againe before they were deſcried, that we could not ſpeake with them.

Sunday the 4. of *February*, was very wett and rainie, with the greateſt guſts of winde that ever we had ſince wee came forth, that though we rid in a very good harbour, yet we were in danger, becauſe our Ship was light, the goods taken out, and ſhe vnballaſed ; and it cauſed much daubing of our houſes to fall downe.

Fryday the 9. ſtill the cold weather continued, that wee could doe little worke. That after-noone our little houſe for our ſicke people was ſet on fire by a ſparke that kindled in the roofe, but no great harme was done. That evening the maſter going aſhore, killed fiue Geeſe, which he friendly diſtributed among the ſicke people ; he found alſo a good Deere killed, the Savages had cut off the hornes, and a Wolfe was eating of him, how he came there we could not conceiue.

Friday the 16. day, was a faire day, but the northerly wind continued, which continued the froſt, this day after-noone one of our people being a fouling, and having taken a ſtand by a creeke ſide in the Reeds, about a myle and an halfe from our Plantation, there came by him twelue *Indians*, marching towards our Plantation, & in the woods he heard the noyſe of many more, he lay cloſe till they were paſſed, and then with what ſpeed he could he went home & gaue the Alarm, ſo the people abroad in the woods returned & armed themſelues, but ſaw none of them, onely toward the euening they made a great fire, about the place where they were firſt diſcovered : Captaine *Miles Standiſh*, and *Francis Cooke*, being at worke in the Woods, comming home, left their

o

tooles

tooles behind them, but before they returned, their tooles were taken away by the Savages. This comming of the Savages gaue vs occasion to keepe more strict watch, and to make our peeces and furniture readie, which by the moysture and rayne were out of temper.

Saturday the 17 day, in the morning we called a meeting for the establishing of military Orders amongst our selues, and we chose *Miles Standish* our Captaine, and gaue him authoritie of command in affayres: and as we were in consultation here abouts, two Savages presented themselues vpon the top of an hill, ouer against our Plantation, about a quarter of a myle and lesse, and made signes vnto vs to come vnto them; we likewise made signes vnto them to come to vs, whereupon we armed our selues, and stood readie, and sent two ouer the brooke towards them, to wit, Captaine *Standish* and *Steven Hopkins*, who went towards them, onely one of them had a Musket, which they layd downe on the ground in their sight, in signe of peace, and to parley with them, but the Savages would not tarry their comming: a noyse of a great many more was heard behind the hill, but no more came in sight. This caused vs to plant our great Ordinances in places most convenient.

Wednesday the 21. of *February*, the master came on shore with many of his Saylers, and brought with him one of the great Peeces, called a *Minion*, and helped vs to draw it vp the hill, with another Peece that lay on shore, and mounted them, and a saller and two bases; he brought with him a very fat Goose to eate with vs, and we had a fat Crane, and a Mallerd, and a dry'd neats-tongue, and so wee were kindly and friendly together.

Saturday the third of *March*, the winde was South, the morning mistie, but towards noone warme and fayre weather; the Birds sang in the Woods most pleasantly; at one of the Clocke it thundred, which was the first wee heard in that Countrey; it was strong and great claps, but short, but after an houre it rayned very sadly till midnight.

Wednesday the seaventh of *March*, the wind was full East, cold,

cold, but faire, that day Mafter *Carver* with fiue other went to the great Ponds, which feeme to be excellent fifhing-places ; all the way they went they found it exceedingly beaten and haunted with Deere, but they faw none; amongft other foule, they faw one a milke white foule, with a very blacke head : this day fome garden feeds were fowen.

Fryday the 16. a fayre warme day towards; this morning we determined to conclude of the military Orders, which we had began to confider of before, but were interrupted by the Savages, as we mentioned formerly ; and whilft we were bufied here about, we were interrupted againe, for there prefented himfelfe a *Savage*, which caufed an Alarm, he very boldly came all alone and along the houfes ftraight to the Randevous, where we intercepted him, not fuffering him to goe in, as vndoubtedly he would, out of his boldneffe, hee faluted vs in Englifh, and bad vs well-come, for he had learned fome broken Englifh amongft the Englifh men that came to fifh at *Monchiggon*, and knew by name the moft of the Captaines, Commanders, & Mafters, that vfually come, he was a man free in fpeech, fo farre as he could expreffe his minde, and of a feemely carriage, we queftioned him of many things, he was the firft *Savage* we could meete withall ; he fayd he was not of thefe parts, but of *Morattiggon*, and one of the *Sagamores* or *Lords* thereof, and had beene 8. moneths in thefe parts, it lying hence a dayes fayle with a great wind, and fiue dayes by land; he difcourfed of the whole Country, and of every Province, and of their *Sagamores*, and their number of men, and ftrength ; the wind beginning to rife a little, we caft a horfemans coat about him, for he was ftarke naked, onely a leather about his waft, with a fringe about a fpan long, or little more ; he had a bow & 2 arrowes, the one headed, and the other vnheaded ; he was a tall ftraight man, the haire of his head blacke, long behind, onely fhort before, none on his face at all ; he asked fome beere, but we gaue him ftrong water, and bisket, and butter, and cheefe, & pudding, and a peece of a mallerd, all which he liked well, and had bin acquainted with fuch amongft the Englifh ; he told vs the

                                                              place

place where we now liue, is called, *Patuxet*, and that about foure yeares agoe, all the Inhabitants dyed of an extraordinary plague, and there is neither man, woman, nor childe remaining, as indeed we haue found none, so as there is none to hinder our possession, or to lay claime vnto it; all the afternoone we spent in communication with him, we would gladly haue beene rid of him at night, but he was not willing to goe this night, then we thought to carry him on ship-boord, wherewith he was well content, and went into the Shallop, but the winde was high and water scant, that it could not returne backe: we lodged him that night at *Steven Hopkins* house, and watched him; the next day he went away backe to the *Masasoits*, from whence he sayd he came, who are our next bordering neighbours: they are sixtie strong, as he sayth: the *Nausites* are as neere South-east of them, and are a hundred strong, and those were they of whom our people were encountred, as we before related. They are much incensed and provoked against the English, and about eyght moneths agoe slew three English men, and two more hardly escaped by flight to *Monhiggon*; they were Sir *Ferdinando Gorge* his men, as this Savage told vs, as he did likewise of the *Huggerie*, that is, *Fight*, that our discoverers had with the *Nausites*, & of our tooles that were taken out of the woods, which we willed him should be brought againe, otherwise, we would right our selues. These people are ill affected towards the English, by reason of one *Hunt*, a master of a ship, who deceived the people, and got them vnder colour of truking with them, twentie out of this very place where we inhabite, and seaven men from the *Nausites*, and carried them away, and sold them for slaues, like a wretched man (for 20. pound a man) that cares not what mischiefe he doth for his profit.

　　Saturday in the morning we dismissed the Salvage, and gaue him a knife, a bracelet, and a ring; he promised within a night or two to come againe, and to bring with him some of the *Massasoyts* our neighbours, with such Beuers skins as they had to trucke with vs.

G

Saturday and Sunday reasonable fayre dayes. On this day
came againe the Savage, and brought with him fiue other
tall proper men, they had euery man a Deeres skin on him,
and the principall of them had a wild Cats skin, or such like
on the one arme ; they had most of them long hosen vp to
their groynes, close made ; and aboue their groynes to their
wast another leather, they were altogether like the *Irish*-trou-
ses;they are of complexion like our English Gipseys no haire
or very little on their faces, on their heads long haire to their
shoulders, onely cut before some trussed vp before with a
feather, broad wise, like a fanne, another a fox tayle hanging
out : these left (according to our charge giuen him before)
their Bowes and Arrowes a quarter of a myle from our
Towne, we gaue them entertaynement as we thought was
fitting them, they did eate liberally of our English victuals,
they made semblance vnto vs of friendship and amitie ; they
song & danced after their maner like Anticks;they brought
with them in a thing like a Bow-case(which the principall of
them had about his wast) a little of their Corne pownded to
Powder, which put to a little water they eate ; he had a little
Tobacco in a bag, but none of them drunke but when he li-
sted, some of them had their faces paynted blacke, from the
forehead to the chin, foure or fiue fingers broad ; others after other fashions, as they liked ; they brought three or foure
skins, but we would not trucke with them at all that day, but
wished them to bring more, and we would trucke for all,
which they promised within a night or two, and would leaue
these behind them, though we were not willing they should,
and they brought vs all our tooles againe which were taken
in the Woods, in our mens absence, so because of the day we
dismissed them so soone as we could. But *Samoset* our first
acquaintance, eyther was sicke, or fayned himselfe so, and
would not goe with them, and stayed with vs till Wednesday
morning : Then we sent him to them, to know the reason
they came not according to their words, and we gaue him an
hat, a payre of stockings and shooes, a shirt, and a peece of
cloth to tie about his wast.

o

The

The Sabboth day, when we sent them from vs, wee gaue every one of them some trifles, especially, the principall of them, we carried them along with our Armes to the place where they left their Bowes and Arrowes, whereat they were amazed, and two of them began to slinke away, but that the other called them, when they tooke their Arrowes, we bad them farewell, and they were glad, and so with many thankes giuen vs they departed, with promise they would come againe.

Munday and tuesday proved fayre dayes, we digged our grounds, and sowed our garden seeds.

Wednesday a fine warme day, we sent away *Samoset*.

That day we had againe a meeting, to conclude of lawes and orders for our selues, and to confirme those Military Orders that were formerly propounded, and twise broken off by the Savages comming, but so we were againe the third time, for after we had beene an houre together, on the top of the hill over against vs two or three Savages presented themselues, that made semblance of daring vs, as we thought, so Captaine *Standish* with another, with their Muskets went over to them, with two of the masters mates that follows them without Armes, having two Muskets with them, they whetted and rubbed their Arrowes and Strings, and made shew of defiance, but when our men drew nere them, they ranne away. Thus we were againe interrupted by them ; this day with much adoe we got our Carpenter that had beene long sicke of the scurvey, to fit our Shallop, to fetch all from aboord.

Thursday the 22. of *March*, was a very fayre warme day. About noone we met againe about our publique businesse, but we had scarce beene an houre together, but *Samoset* came againe, and *Squanto* the onely natiue of *Patuxat*, where we now inhabite, who was one of the twentie Captiues that by *Hunt* were carried away, and had beene in *England*, & dwelt in *Cornehill* with master *Iohn Slanie* a Marchant, and could speake a little English, with three others, and they brought with them some few skinnes to trucke, and some red Herrings

rings newly taken and dryed, but not salted, and signified vnto vs, that their great Sagamore *Masasoyt* was hard by, with *Quadequina* his brother, and all their men. They could not well expresse in English what they would, but after an houre the King came to the top of an hill over against vs, and had in his trayne sixtie men, that wee could well behold them, and they vs: we were not willing to send our governour to them, and they vnwilling to come to vs, so *Squanto* went againe vnto him, who brought word that wee should send one to parley with him, which we did, which was *Edward Winsloe*, to know his mind, and to signifie the mind and will of our governour, which was to haue trading and peace with him. We sent to the King a payre of Kniues, and a Copper Chayne, with a Iewell at it. To *Quadequina* we sent likewise a Knife and a Iewell to hang in his eare, and withall a Pot of strong water, a good quantitie of Bisket, and some butter, which were all willingly accepted: our Messenger made a speech vnto him, that King IAMES saluted him with words of loue and Peace, and did accept of him as his Friend and Alie, and that our Governour desired to see him and to trucke with him, and to confirme a Peace with him, as his next neighbour: he liked well of the speech and heard it attentiuely, though the Interpreters did not well expresse it; after he had eaten and drunke himselfe, and giuen the rest to his company, he looked vpon our messengers sword and armour which he had on, with intimation of his desire to buy it, but on the other side, our messenger shewed his vnwillingnes to part with it: In the end he left him in the custodie of *Quadequina* his brother, and came ouer the brooke, and some twentie men following him, leaving all their Bowes and Arrowes behind them. We kept six or seauen as hostages for our messenger; Captaine *Standish* and master *Williamson* met the King at the brooke, with halfe a dosen Musketiers, they saluted him and he them, so one going over, the one on the one side, and the other on the other, conducted him to an house then in building, where we placed a greene Rugge, and three or foure Cushions, then instantly came our

Gover-

Governour with Drumme and Trumpet after him, and some few Musketiers. After salutations, our Governour kissing his hand, the King kissed him, and so they sat downe. The Governour called for some strong water, and drunke to him, and he drunke a great draught that made him sweate all the while after, he called for a little fresh meate, which the King did eate willingly, and did giue his followers. Then they treated of Peace, which was;

1. That neyther he nor any of his should iniure or doe hurt to any of our people.

2. And if any of his did hurt to any of ours, he should send the offender, that we might punish him.

The agreements of peace betweene vs and Massasoyt.

3. That if any of our Tooles were taken away when our people were at worke, he should cause them to be restored, and if ours did any harme to any of his, wee would doe the like to them.

4. If any did vniustly warre against him, we would ayde him; If any did warre against vs, he should ayde vs.

5. He should send to his neighbour Confederates, to certifie them of this, that they might not wrong vs, but might be likewise comprised in the conditions of Peace.

6. That when their men came to vs, they should leaue their Bowes and Arrowes behind them, as wee should doe our Peeces when we came to them.

Lastly, that doing thus, King IAMES would esteeme of him as his friend and Alie: all which the King seemed to like well, and it was applauded of his followers, all the while he sat by the Governour he trembled for feare: In his person he is a very lustie man, in his best yeares, an able body, graue of countenance, and spare of speech: In his Attyre little or nothing differing from the rest of his followers, only in a great Chaine of white bone Beades about his necke, and at it behinde his necke, hangs a little bagg of Tobacco, which he dranke and gaue vs to drinke; his face was paynted with a sad red like murry, and oyled both head and face, that hee looked greasily: All his followers likewise, were in their faces, in part or in whole painted, some blacke, some red

red, some yellow, and some white, some with crosses, and other Antick workes, some had skins on them, and some naked, all strong, tall, all men in appearance: so after all was done, the Governour conducted him to the Brooke, and there they embraced each other and he departed: we diligently keeping our hostages, wee expected our messengers comming, but anon word was brought vs, that *Quaddequina* was comming, and our messenger was stayed till his returne, who presently came and a troupe with him, so likewise wee entertained him, and convayed him to the place prepared; he was very fearefull of our peeces, and made signes of dislike, that they should be carried away, whereupon Commandement was given, they should be layd away. He was a very proper tall young man, of a very modest and seemely countenance, and he did kindely like of our entertainement, so we convayed him likewise as wee did the King, but diuers of their people stayed still, when hee was returned, then they dismissed our messenger. Two of his people would haue stayed all night, but we would not suffer it: one thing I forgot, the King had in his bosome hanging in a string, a great long knife, hee marveiled much at our Trumpet, and some of his men would sound it as well as they could, *Samoset* and *Squanto*, they stayed al night with vs, and the King and al his men lay all night in the woods, not aboue halfe an English myle from vs, and all their wiues and women with them, they sayd that within 8. or 9. dayes, they would come and set corne on the other side of the Brooke, and dwell there all Summer, which is hard by vs: That night we kept good watch, but there was no appearance of danger; the next morning divers of their people came over to vs, hoping to get some victuales as wee imagined, som of them told vs the King would haue some of vs come see him; Captaine *Standish* and *Isaack Alderton* went venterously, who were welcommed of him after their manner: he gaue them three or foure ground Nuts, and some Tobacco. Wee cannot yet conceiue, but that he is willing to haue peace with vs, for they haue seene our people sometimes alone two or three in

the

the woods at worke and fowling, when as they offered them
no harme as they might eafily haue done., and efpecially
becaufe hee hath a potent Adverfary the _Narowhiganfeis,_
that are at warre with him, againft whom hee thinkes wee
may be fome ftrength to him, for our peeces are terrible vnto them; this morning, they ftayed till ten or eleuen of the
Clocke, and our Governour bid them fend the Kings kettle,
and filled it full of peafe, which pleafed them well, and fo
they went their way.

Fryday was a very faire day, _Samofet_ and _Squanto_ ftill remained with vs, _Squanto_ went at noone to fifh for Eeles, at
night he came home with as many as he could well lift in one
hand, which our people were glad of, they were fat & fweet,
he trod them out with his feete, and fo caught them with his
hands without any other Inftrument,

This day we proceeded on with our common bufineffe,
from which we had beene fo often hindred by the Salvages
comming, and concluded both of Military orders,
and of fome Lawes and Orders as wee thought be-
hoofefull for our prefent eftate, and condition,
and did likewife choofe our Governour for
this yeare, which was Mafter _Iohn_
Carver a man well approo-
ved amongft vs.

A

A
IOVRNEY TO *PACKANOKIK*,
The Habitation of the Great King
MASSASOYT.
As alfo our Meſſage, the
Anſwere and intertaine-
ment wee had of
H I M.

IT ſeemed good to the Company for ma-
ny conſiderations to ſend ſome amongſt
them to *Maſſaſoyt*, the greateſt Commander amongſt the Savages, bordering about vs; partly to know where to
find them, if occaſion ſerved, as alſo to
ſee their ſtrength, diſcover the Country,
prevent abuſes in their diſorderly comming vnto vs, make
ſatisfaction for ſome conceived jniuries to be done on our
parts, and to continue the league of Peace and Friendſhip
betweene them and vs. For theſe, and the like ends, it pleaſed
the Governour to make choice of *Steven Hopkins*, & *Edward
Winſlow* to goe vnto him, and having a fit opportunitie, by
reaſon of a Savage, called *Tiſquantum* (that could ſpeake
Engliſh) comming vnto vs; with all expedition provided a
Horſe-mans coat, of red Cotton, and laced with a ſlight lace
for a preſent, that both they and their meſſage might be the
more acceptable amongſt them. The Meſſage was as fol-
loweth; That foraſmuch as his ſubiects came often and
without feare, vpon all occaſions amongſt vs, ſo wee were
now come vnto him, and in witneſſe of the loue and
good will the Engliſh beare vnto him, the Governour hath
ſent him a coat, deſiring that the Peace and Amitie that was
be-

betweene them and vs might be continued, not that we feared them, but becaufe we intended not to iniure any, defiring to liue peaceably : and as with all men, fo efpecially with them our neereft neighbours. But whereas his people came very often, and very many together vnto vs, bringing for the moft part their wiues and children with them, they were well come ; yet we being but ftrangers as yet at *Patuxet, alias New Plimmoth,* and not knowing how our Corne might profper, we could no longer giue them fuch entertainment as we had done, and as we defired ftill to doe: yet if he would be pleafed to come himfelfe, or any fpeciall friend of his defired to fee vs, comming from him they fhould be well-come ; and to the end wee might know them from others, our Governour had fent him a copper Chayne, defiring if any Meffenger fhould come from him to vs, we might know him by bringing it with him, and hearken and giue credite to his Meffage accordingly. Alfo requefting him that fuch as haue skins, fhould bring them to vs, and that he would hinder the multitude from oppreffing vs with them. And whereas at our firft arriuall at *Paomet* (called by vs *Cape Cod*) we found there Corne buried in the ground, and finding no inhabitants but fome graues of dead new buryed, tooke the Corne, refolving if ever we could heare of any that had right thereunto, to make fatisfaction to the full for it, yet fince we vnderftand the owners thereof were fled for feare of vs, our defire was either to pay them with the like quantitie of corne, Englifh meale, or any other Commodities we had to pleafure them withall ; requefting him that fome one of his men might fignifie fo much vnto them, and wee would content him for his paines. And laft of all, our Gouernour requefted one fauour of him, which was, that he would exchange fome of their Corne for feede with us, that we might make tryall which beft agreed with the foyle where we liue.

With thefe prefents and meffage we fet forward the tenth Iune, about 9. a clocke in the Morning, our guide refolving that night to reft at *Namafchet,* a Towne vnder *Maffafoyt,* and conceived by vs to bee very neere, becaufe the

Inhabitants flocked so thicke vpon every slight occasion a-
mongst vs: but wee found it to bee some fifteene English
myles. On the way we found some ten or twelue men women and children, which had pestered vs, till wee were wearie of them, perceiving that (as the manner of them all is)
where victuall is easiliest to be got, there they liue, especially
in the Summer : by reason whereof our Bay affording many Lobsters, they resort every spring tide thither: & now returned with vs to *Namaschet*. Thither we came about 3. a
clock after noone, the Inhabitants entertaining vs with ioy,
in the best manner they could, giving vs a kinde of bread called by them *Maizium*, and the spawne of Shads, which then
they got in abundance, in so much as they gaue vs spoones
to eate them, with these they boyled mustie Acorns, but
of the Shads we eate heartily. After this they desired one of
our men to shoote at a Crow, complaining what damage
they sustained in their Corne by them, who shooting some
fourescore off and killing, they much admired it, as other
shots on other occasions. After this *Tisquantum* told vs we
should hardly in one day reach *Pakanokick*, moving vs to
goe some 8. myles further, where we should finde more store
and better victuals then there : Being willing to hasten our
Iourney we went, and came thither at Sunne setting, where
we found many of the *Namaschezcks* (they so calling the men
of *Namaschet*) fishing vppon a Ware which they had made
on a River which belonged to them, where they caught a-
bundance of Basse. These welcommed vs also, gaue vs of
their fish, and we them of our victuals, not doubting but we
should haue enough where ere we came. There we lodged
in the open fieldes : for houses they had none, though they
spent the most of the Summer there. The head of this River is reported to bee not farre from the place of our abode,
vpon it are, and haue beene many Townes, it being a good
length. The ground is very good on both sides, it being for
the most part cleered : Thousands of men haue lived there,
which dyed in a great plague not long since : and pitty it was
and is to see, so many goodly fieldes, & so well seated, with-
                                                          out

out men to dreſſe and manure the ſame. Vppon this River dwelleth *Maſſaſoyt* : It commeth into the Sea at the *Narrohiganſet* Bay, where the French men ſo much vſe. A ſhipp may goe many myles vp it, as the Salvages report, and a ſhallop to the head of it : but ſo farre as wee ſaw, wee are ſure a Shallop may.

But to returne to our Iourney. The next morning wee brake our faſt, tooke our leaue and departed, being then accompanied with ſome ſixe Salvages, having gone about ſixe myles by the River ſide, at a knowne ſhole place, it beeing low water, they ſpake to vs to put off our breeches, for wee muſt wade thorow. Heere let me not forget the vallour and courrage of ſome of the Salvages, on the oppoſite ſide of the river, for there were remaining aliue only 2. men, both aged, eſpecially the one being aboue threeſcore ; Theſe two eſpying a company of men entring the River, ran very ſwiftly & low in the graſſe to meete vs at the banck, where with ſhrill voyces and great courage ſtanding charged vppon vs with their bowes, they demaunded what we were, ſuppoſing vs to be enemies, and thinking to take advantage on vs in the water : but ſeeing we were friends, they welcommed vs with ſuch foode as they had, and we beſtowed a ſmall bracelet of Beades on them. Thus farre wee are ſure the Tide ebs and flowes.

Having here againe refreſhed our ſelves, we proceeded in our Iourney, the weather being very hote for travell, yet the Country ſo well watered, that a man could ſcarce be drie, but he ſhould haue a ſpring at hand to coole his thirſt, beſide ſmal Rivers in abundance : But the Salvages will not willingly drinke, but at a ſpring head. When wee came to any ſmall Brooke where no bridge was, two of them deſired to carry vs through of their owne accords, alſo fearing wee were or would be weary, offered to carry our peeces, alſo if we would lay off any of our clothes, we ſhould haue them carried : and as the one of them had found more ſpeciall kindneſſe from one of the Meſſengers, and the other Salvage from the other ſo they ſhewed their thankefulneſſe accordingly in affording vs all helpe, and furtherance in the Iourney.

As we passed along, we observed that there were few places by the River, but had beene inhabited, by reason whereof, much ground was cleare, saue of weedes which grewe higher then our heads. There is much good Timber both Oake, Walnut-tree, Firre, Beech, and exceeding great Chessnut-trees. The Country in respect of the lying of it, is both Champanie and hilly, like many places in England. In some places its very rockie both aboue ground and in it: And though the Countrey bee wilde and over-growne with woods, yet the trees stand not thicke, but a man may well ride a horse amongst them.

Passing on at length, one of the Company an *Indian* espied a man, and told the rest of it, we asked them if they feared any, they told vs that if they were *Narrohigganset*, men they would not trust them, whereat, we called for our peeces and bid them not to feare ; for though they were twenty, we two alone would not care for them : but they hayling him, hee prooved a friend, and had onely two women with him: their baskets were empty, but they fetched water in their bottels, so that we dranke with them and departed. After we met another man with other two women, which had beene at Randevow by the salt water, and their baskets were full of rosted Crab-fishes, and other dryed shell fish, of which they gaue vs, and wee eate and dranke with them: and gaue each of the women a string of Beades, and departed.

After wee came to a Towne of *Massasoyts*, where we eat Oysters and other fish. From thence we went to *Packanokick*, but *Massasoyt* was not at home, there we stayed, he being sent for: when newes was brought of his comming, our guide *Tisquantum* requested that at our meeting, wee would discharge our peeces, but one of vs going about to charge his peece, the women and children through feare to see him take vpp his peece, ran away, and could not bee pacified, till hee layd it downe againe, who afterward were better informed by our Interpreter.

Massasoyt being come, wee discharged our Peeces, and faluted saluted him, who after their manner kindly well commed vs, and tooke vs into his house, and set vs downe by him, where having delivered our foresayd Message, and Presents, and having put the Coat on his backe, and the Chayne about his necke, he was not a little proud to behold himselfe, and his men also to see their King so brauely attyred.

For answere to our Message, he told vs we were well-come, and he would gladly continue that Peace and Friendship which was betweene him & vs: and for his men they should no more pester vs as they had done: Also, that he would send to *Paomet*, and would helpe vs with Corne for seed, according to our request.

This being done, his men gathered neere to him, to whom he turned himselfe, and made a great Speech; they sometime interposing, and as it were, confirming and applauding him in that he sayd. The meaning whereof was (as farre as we could learne) thus; Was not he *Massasoyt* Commander of the Countrey about them? Was not such a Towne his and the people of it? and should they not bring their skins vnto vs? To which they answered, they were his & would be at peace with vs, and bring their skins to vs. After this manner, he named at least thirtie places, and their answere was as aforesayd to euery one: so that as it was delightfull, it was tedious vnto vs.

This being ended, he lighted Tobacco for vs, and fell to discoursing of *England*, & of the Kings Maiestie, marvayling that he would liue without a wife. Also he talked of the French-men, bidding vs not to suffer them to come to *Narrohiganset*, for it was King I A M E S his Countrey, and he also was King I A M E S his man. Late it grew, but victualls he offered none; for indeed he had not any, being he came so newly home. So we desired to goe to rest: he layd vs on the bed with himselfe and his wife, they at the one end and we at the other, it being onely plancks layd a foot from the ground, and a thin Mat vpon them. Two more of his chiefe men for want of roome pressed by and vpon vs; so that we were worse weary of our lodging then of our iourney.

The

The next day being Thurſday, many of their Sachims, or petty Governours came to ſee vs, and many of their men alſo. There they went to their manner of Games for skins and kniues. There we challenged them to ſhoote with them for skins : but they durſt not : onely they deſired to ſee one of vs ſhoote at a marke, who ſhooting with Haile-ſhot, they wondred to ſee the marke ſo full of holes. About one a clocke, _Maſſaſoyt_ brought two fiſhes that he had ſhot, they were like Breame but three times ſo bigge, and better meate. Theſe being boyled there were at leſt fortie looked for ſhare in them, the moſt eate of them : This meale onely we had in two nights and a day, and had not one of vs bought a Partridge, we had taken our Iourney faſting : Very importunate he was to haue vs ſtay with them longer : But wee deſired to keepe the Sabboth at home : and feared we ſhould either bè light-headed for want of ſleepe, for what with bad lodging, the Savages barbarous ſinging, (for they vſe to ſing themſelues aſleepe) lice and fleas within doores, and Muskeetoes without, wee could hardly ſleepe all the time of our being there ; we much fearing, that if wee ſhould ſtay any longer, we ſhould not be able to recover home for want of ſtrength. So that on the Fryday morning before Sun-riſing, we tooke our leaue and departed, _Maſſaſoyt_ being both grieved and aſhamed, that he could no better entertaine vs: and retaining _Tiſquantum_ to ſend from place to place to procure trucke for vs: and appointing another, called _Tokamahamon_ in his place, whom we had found faithfull before and after vpon all occaſions.

At this towne of _Maſſaſoyts_, where we before eate, wee were againe refreſhed with a little fiſh ; and bought about a handfull of Meale of their parched Corne, which was very precious at that time of the yeere, and a ſmall ſtring of dryed ſhell-fiſh, as big as Oyſters. The latter we gaue to the ſixe Savages that accompanied vs, keeping the Meale for our ſelues, when we dranke we eate each a ſpoonefull of it with a Pipe of Tobacco, in ſtead of other victuals ; and of this alſo we could not but giue them ſo long as it laſted, Fiue myles
they

they led vs to a houfe out of the way in hope of victualls: but we found no body there, and fo were but worfe able to returne home. That night we reached to the wire where we lay before, but the *Namafchencks* were returned: fo that we had no hope of any thing there. One of the Savages had fhot a Shad in the water, and a fmall Squirrill as big as a Rat, called a *Neuxis*, the one halfe of either he gaue vs, and after went to the wire to fifh. From hence we wrote to *Plimouth*, and fent *Tokamahamon* before to *Namasket*, willing him from thence to fend another, that he might meet vs with food at *Namasket*. Two men now onely remained with vs, and it pleafed God to giue them good ftore of fifh, fo that we were well refrefhed. After fupper we went to reft, and they to fifhing againe : more they gat and fell to eating a-frefh, and retayned fufficient readie roft for all our break-fafts. About two a Clocke in the morning, arofe a great ftorme of wind, raine, lightning, and thunder, in fuch violent manner, that we could not keepe in our fire ; and had the Savages not rofted fifh when we were afleepe, we had fet forward fafting : for the raine ftill continued with great violence, even the whole day thorow, till wee came within two myles of home.

Being wett and weary, at length we came to *Namafchet*, there we refrefhed our felues, giuing gifts to all fuch as had fhewed vs any kindneffe. Amongft others one of the fixe that came with vs from *Packanokik*, having before this on the way vnkindly forfaken vs, marvayled we gaue him nothing, and told vs what he had done for vs ; we alfo told him of fome difcurtefies he offered vs, whereby he deferved nothing, yet we gaue him a fmall trifle : wherevpon he offered vs Tobacco : but the houfe being full of people, we told them hee ftole fome by the way, and if it were of that we would not take it : For we would not receiue that which was ftolne vpon any termes ; if we did, our God would be angry with vs, and deftroy vs. This abafhed him, and gaue the reft great content : but at our departure he would needs carry him on his backe thorow a River, whom he had formerly in fome

fort

fort abuſed. Faine they would haue had vs to lodge there
all night : and wondered we would ſet forth againe in
ſuch Weather : but GOD be prayſed, wee
came ſafe home that night, though
wett, weary, and
ſurbated.

A

A
VOYAGE MADE BY TEN
of our Men to the Kingdome of
N A V S E T, to feeke a Boy that had
loft himfelfe in the WOODS;
With fuch Accidents as
befell vs in that
VOYAGE.

He 11th of *Iune* we fet forth, the weather
being very faire : but ere we had bin long
at Sea, there arofe a ftorme of wind and
raine, with much lightning and thunder,
in fo much that a fpout arofe not far from
vs : but God be prayfed, it dured not long,
and we put in that night for Harbour at a
place, called *Cummaquid*, where wee had fome hope to
finde the Boy. Two Savages were in the Boat with vs, the
one was *Tifquantum* our Interpreter, the other *Tokamahamon*,
a fpeciall friend. It being night before we came in, we Anchored in the middeft of the Bay, where we were drie at a
low water. In the morning we efpied Savages feeking Lobfters, and fent our two Interpreters to fpeake with them, the
channell being betweene them ; where they told them what
we were, and for what we were come, willing them not at all
to feare vs, for we would not hurt them. Their anfwere was,
that the Boy was well, but he was at *Naufet* ; yet fince wee
were there they defired vs to come afhore & eate with them :
Which as foone as our Boat floated we did : and went fixe a-
fhore, having foure pledges for them in the Boate. They
brought vs to their Sachim or Gouernour, whom they call

I   *Iyanough,*

Iyanough, a man not exceeding twentie-six yeeres of age, but very personable, gentle, courteous, and fayre conditioned, indeed not like a Savage, saue for his attyre; his entertainement was answerable to his parts, and his cheare plentifull and various.

One thing was very grieuous vnto vs at this place; There was an old woman, whom we iudged to be no lesse then an hundred yeeres old, which came to see vs because shee neuer saw English, yet could not behold vs without breaking forth into great passion, weeping and crying excessiuely. We demaunding the reason of it, they told vs, shee had three sons, who when master *Hunt* was in these parts went aboord his Ship to trade with him, and he carried them Captiues into Spaine (for *Tisquantum* at that time was carried away also) by which meanes shee was depriued of the comfort of her children in her old age. We told them we were sorry that any English man should giue them that offence, that *Hunt* was a bad man, and that all the English that heard of it condemned him for the same: but for vs we would not offer them any such iniury, though it would gaine vs all the skins in the Countrey. So we gaue her some small trifles, which somewhat appeased her.

After dinner we tooke Boat for *Nauset, Iyanough* and two of his men accompanying vs, Ere we came to *Nauset*, the day and tyde were almost spent, in so much as we could not goe in with our Shallop: but the Sachim or Gouernour of *Commaquid* went a shore and his men with him, we also sent *Tisquantum* to tell *Aspinet* the Sachim of *Nauset* wherefore we came. The Sauages here came very thicke amongst vs, and were earnest with vs to bring in our Boate. But we neither well could, nor yet desired to doe it, because we had lesse cause to trust them, being they onely had formerly made an Assault vpon vs in the same place, in time of our Winter Discouery for Habitation. And indeed it was no matuayle they did so, for: howsoeuer through snow or otherwise wee saw no houses, yet wee were in the middest of them.

i   When

When our boat was aground they came very thicke, but wee stood therein vpon our guard, not suffering any to enter except two: the one being of *Maramoick*, and one of those, whose Corne we had formerly found, we promised him restitution, & desired him either to come to *Patuxet* for satisfaction, or else we would bring them so much corne againe, hee promised to come, wee vsed him very kindely for the present. Some few skins we gate there but not many.

After Sun-set, *Aspinet* came with a great traine, & brought the boy with him, one bearing him through the water: hee had not lesse then an hundred with him, the halfe whereof came to the Shallop side vnarmed with him, the other stood aloofe with their bow and arrowes. There he delivered vs the boy, behung with beades, and made peace with vs, wee bestowing a knife on him, and likewise on another that first entertained the Boy and brought him thither. So they departed from vs.

Here we vnderstood, that the *Narrohigansets* had spoyled some of *Massasoyts* men, and taken him. This strucke some feare in vs, because the Colony was so weakely guarded, the strength thereof being abroad: But we set foorth with resolution to make the best hast home wee could; yet the winde being contrary, having scarce any fresh water leaft, and at least. 16. leagues home, we put in againe for the shore. There we met againe with *Iyanough* the *Sachim* of *Cúmaquid*, and the most of his Towne, both men women & children with him. Hee being still willing to gratifie vs, tooke a runlet and led our men in the darke a great way for water, but could finde none good: yet brought such as there was on his necke with them. In the meane time the women ioyned hand in hand, singing and dancing before the Shallop, the men also shewing all the kindnes they could, *Iyanough* himselfe taking a bracelet from about his necke, and hanging it vpon one of vs.

Againe we set out but to small purpose: for wee gat but little homeward; Our water also was very brackish, and not to be drunke.

　　　　The

The next morning, *Iyanough* eſpied vs againe and ran after vs ; we being reſolved to goe to *Cummaquid* againe to water, tooke him into the Shallop, whoſe entertainement was not inferiour vnto the former.

The ſoyle at *Nauſet* and here is alike, even and ſandy, not ſo good for corne as where wee are ; Shipps may ſafely ride in eyther harbour. In the Summer, they abound with fiſh. Being now wa-tered, we put forth againe, and by Gods providence, came ſafely home that night.

(*⁎*)

A

A IOVRNEY TO THE
Kingdome of *NAMASCHET*
in defence of the Great King
MASSASOYT *against the Nar-*
rohigganſets, and to revenge
the ſuppoſed Death
of our Interpreter
Tiſquantum.

T our returne from *Nauſet,* we found it true, that *Maſſaſoyt* was put from his Countrey by the *Narrohigganſets.* Word alſo was brought vnto vs, that one *Coubatant* a petty Sachim or Governour vnder *Maſſaſoyt* (whom they euer feared to be too conver-ſant with the *Narrohigganſets*) was at *Namaſchet,* who ſought to draw the hearts of *Maſſaſoyts* ſubieets from him, ſpeaking alſo diſdainfully of vs, ſtorming at the Peace be-tweene *Nauſet, Cummaquid,* and vs, and at *Tiſquantum* the worker of it ; alſo at *Tokamahamon,* and one *Hobbamock* (two Indians or Lemes, one of which he would trecherouſly haue murdered a little before, being a ſpeciall and truſty man of *Maſſaſoyts*) *Tokamahamon* went to him, but the other two would not ; yet put their liues in their hands, priuately went to ſee if they could heare of their King, and lodging at *Na-maſchet* were diſcouered to *Coubatant,* who ſet a guard to be-ſet the houſe and tooke *Tiſquantum* (for he had ſayd, if he were dead, the Engliſh had loſt their tongue) *Hobbamock* ſee-ing that *Tiſquantum* was taken, and *Coubatant* held a knife at his breaſt, being a ſtrong and ſtout man, brake from them and came to *New-Plimmouth,* full of feare and ſorrow for *Tiſquantum,* whom he thought to be ſlaine.

Vpon

Vpon this Newes the Company aſſembled together, and reſolued on the morrow to ſend ten men armed to *Namaſchet* and *Hobbamock*, for their guide, to reuenge the ſuppoſed death of *Tiſquantum* on *Coubatant* our bitter Enemy, and to retaine *Nepeof*, another Sachim or Gouernour, who was of this confederacy, till we heard, what was become of our friend *Maſſaſoyt*.

On the morrow we ſet out ten men Armed, who tooke their iourney as aforeſayd, but the day proued very wett. When wee ſuppoſed we were within three or foure myles of *Namaſchet*, we went out of the way and ſtayed there till night, becauſe we would not be diſcouered. There we conſulted what to doe, and thinking beſt to beſet the houſe at mid-night, each was appointed his taske by the Captaine, all men incouraging one another, to the vtmoſt of their power.

By night our guide loſt his way, which much diſcouraged our men, being we were wet, and weary of our armes: but one of our men hauing beene before at *Namaſchet* brought vs into the way againe.

Before we came to the Towne we ſat downe and ate ſuch as our Knapſacke affoorded, that being done, wee threw them aſide, and all ſuch things as might hinder vs, and ſo went on and beſet the houſe, according to our laſt reſolution. Thoſe that entred, demaunded if *Coubatant* were not there: but feare had bereft the Savages of ſpeech. We charged them not to ſtirre, for if *Coubatant* were not there, we would not meddle with them, if he were, we came principally for him, to be auenged on him for the ſuppoſed death of *Tiſquantum*, and other matters: but howſoeuer wee would not at all hurt their women, or children. Notwithſtanding ſome of them preſſed out at a priuate doore and eſcaped, but with ſome wounds: At length perceiuing our principall ends, they told vs *Coubatant* was returned with all his traine, and that *Tiſquantum* was yet liuing, and in the towne offering ſome Tobacco, other ſuch as they had to eate. In this hurley burley we diſcharged two Peeces at randome, which much

terrified

terrified all the Inhabitants, except *Tisquantum* and *Tokama-hamon*, who though they knew not our end in comming, yet assured them of our honesty, that we would not hurt them. Those boyes that were in the house seeing our care of women, often cryed *Neen squaes*, that is to say, I am a Woman : the Women also hanging vpon *Hobbamock*, calling him *Towam*, that is, Friend. But to be short, we kept them we had, and made them make a fire that we might see to search the house. In the meane time, *Hobbamock* gat on the top of the house, and called *Tisquantum* and *Tokamahamon*, which came vnto vs accompanied with others, some armed and others naked. Those that had Bowes and Arrowes we tooke them away, promising them againe when it was day. The house we tooke for our better safegard : but released those we had taken, manifesting whom we came for and wherefore.

On the next morning we marched into the middest of the Towne, and went to the house of *Tisquantum* to breakfast. Thither came all whose hearts were vpright towardes vs, but all *Coubatants* faction were fled away. There in the middest of them we manifested againe our intendment, assuring them, that although *Coubatant* had now escaped vs, yet there was no place should secure him and his from vs if he continued his threatning vs, and prouoking others against vs, who had kindly entertained him, and neuer intended euill towards him till he now so iustly deserued it. Moreover, if *Massasoyt* did not returne in safetie from *Narrohiganset*, or if hereafter he should make any insurrection against him, or offer violence to *Tisquantum*, *Hobbamock*, or any of *Massasoyts* Subiects, we would revenge it vpon him, to the ouer-throw of him and his. As for those were wounded, we were sorry for it, though themselues procured it in not staying in the house at our command : yet if they would returne home with vs, our Surgeon should heale them.

At this offer, one man and a woman that were wounded went home with vs, *Tisquantum* and many other knowne
friends

friends accompanying vs, and offering all helpe that
might be by carriage of any thing wee had to eafe
vs. So that by Gods good Providence wee
fafely returned home the morrow
night after we fet forth.
(:.*)

A

A
RELATION OF OVR
Voyage to the *MASSACHVSETS*,
And what happened there.

T ſeemed good to the Company in gene-
rall, that though the *Maſſachuſets* had of-
ten threatned vs (as we were informed)
yet we ſhould goe amongſt them, partly
to ſee the Countrey, partly to make
Peace with them, and partly to procure
their trucke.

For theſe ends the Governours choſe ten men, fit for the
purpoſe, and ſent *Tiſquantum*, and two other Salvages to
bring vs to ſpeech with the people, and interpret for vs.

We ſet out about mid-night, the tyde then ſeruing for vs;
we ſuppoſing it to be neerer then it is, thought to be there
the next morning betimes: but it proued well neere twentie
Leagues from *New Plimmouth*.

We came into the bottome of the Bay, but being late wee
anchored and lay in the Shallop, not hauing ſeene any of the
people. The next morning we put in for the ſhore. There
we found many Lobſters that had beene gathered together
by the Saluages, which we made ready vnder a cliffe. The
Captaine ſet two Sentinels behind the cliffe to the landward
to ſecure the Shallop, and taking a guide with him, and foure
of our company, went to ſeeke the Inhabitants, where they
met a woman comming for her Lobſters, they told her of
them, and contented her for them. She told them where the
people were; *Tiſquantum* went to them, the reſt returned,
hauing direction which way to bring the Shallop to them.

The Sachim, or Gouernour of this place, is called *Obba-
tinewat*, and though he liue in the bottome of the *Maſſachu-
ſet* bay, yet he is vnder *Maſſaſoyt*. He vſed vs very kindly;
he told vs, he durſt not then remaine in any ſetled place,
for feare of the *Tarentines*. Alſo the *Squa Sachim*, or *Maſſachuſets* Queene was an enemy to him.

K   We

We told him of diuers Sachims that had acknowledged
themselues to be King I A M E s his men, and if he also would
submit himselfe, we would be his safegard from his enemies;
which he did, and went along with vs to bring vs to the
Squa Sachim: Againe we crossed the Bay which is very large,
and hath at left fiftie Ilands in it: but the certaine number is
not knowne to the Inhabitants. Night it was before wee
came to that side of the Bay where this people were. On shore
the Saluages went but found no body. That night also we
rid at Anchor aboord the Shallop.

On the morrow we went ashore, all but two men, and marched in Armes vp in the Countrey. Hauing gone three
myles, we came to a place where Corne had beene newly
gathered, a house pulled downe, and the people gone. A
myle from hence, *Nanepashemet* their King in his life time
had liued. His house was not like others, but a scaffold was
largely built, with pools and plancks some six foote from
ground, and the house vpon that, being situated on the top
of a hill.

Not farre from hence in a bottome, wee came to a Fort
built by their deceased King, the manner thus; There were
pools some thirtie or fortie foote long, stucke in the ground
as thicke as they could be set one by another, and with these
they inclosed a ring some forty or fifty foote ouer. A trench
breast high was digged on each side; one way there was to
goe into it with a bridge; in the midst of this Pallizado stood
the frame of an house, wherein being dead he lay buryed.

About a myle from hence, we came to such another, but
seated on the top of an hill: here *Nanepashemet* was killed,
none dwelling in it since the time of his death. At this place
we stayed, and sent two Saluages to looke the Inhabitants,
and to informe them of our ends in comming, that they
might not be fearefull of vs: Within a myle of this place
they found the women of the place together, with their
Corne on heapes, whither we supposed them to be fled for
feare of vs, and the more, because in diuers places they had
newly pulled downe their houses; and for hast in one place
had left some of their Corne couered with a Mat, and no body with it.   With

With much feare they entertained vs at firft, but feeing our gentle carriage towards them, they tooke heart and en-tertained vs in the beft manner they could, boyling Cod and fuch other things as they had for vs. At length with much fending for came one of their men, fhaking and trembling for feare. But when he faw we intended them no hurt, but came to trucke, he promifed vs his skins alfo. Of him we enquired for their Queene, but it feemed fhee was far from thence, at left we could not fee her.

Here *Tifquantum* would haue had vs rifled the Saluage women, and taken their skins, and all fuch things as might be feruiceable for vs; for (fayd he) they are a bad people, and haue oft threatned you: But our anfwere was; Were they neuer fo bad, we would not wrong them, or giue them any juft occafion againft vs: for their words we little weighed them, but if they once attempted any thing againft vs, then we would deale far worfe then he defired.

Hauing well fpent the day, we returned to the Shallop, almoft all the Women accompanying vs, to trucke, who fold their coats from their backes, and tyed boughes about them, but with great fhamefaftneffe (for indeed they are more modeft then fome of our Englifh women are) we pro-mifed them to come againe to them, and they vs, to keepe their skins.

Within this Bay, the Salvages fay, there are two Riuers ; the one whereof we faw, hauing a faire entrance, but we had no time to difcouer it. Better harbours for fhipping cannot be then here are. At the entrance of the Bay are many Rockes ; and in all likelihood very good fifhing ground. Many, yea, moft of the Ilands haue beene inhabited, fome being cleered from end to end, but the people are all dead, or remoued.

Our victuall growing fcarce, the Winde comming fayre, and hauing a light Moone, we fet out at euening, and through the goodneffe of
G O D, came fafely home be-
fore noone the day
following.

A

A
LETTER SENT FROM
New-England to a friend in thefe parts,
fetting forth a briefe and true Declaration
of the worth of that Plantation ;
As alfo certaine vfefull Directions
for fuch as intend a V O Y A G E
into thofe Parts.

 Ouing, and old Friend, although
I receiued no Letter from you
by this Ship, yet forafmuch as I
know you expect the perfor-
mance of my promife, which
was, to write vnto you truely
and faithfully of all things. I
haue therefore at this time fent
vnto you accordingly. Refer-
ring you for further fatisfaction
to our more large Relations You fhall vnderftand, that in
this little time, that a few of vs haue beene here, we haue built
feauen dwelling houfes, and foure for the vfe of the Plantation, and haue made preparation for divers others. We fet the
laft Spring fome twentie Acres of *Indian* Corne, and fowed
fome fix Acres of Barly & Peafe, and according to the manner of the *Indians*, we manured our ground with Herings or
rather Shadds, which we haue in great abundance, and take
with great eafe at our doores Our Corne did proue well, &
God be prayfed, we had a good increafe of *Indian* Corne,
and our Barly indifferent good, but our Peafe not worth the
gathering, for we feared they were too late fowne, they
came vp very well, and bloffomed, but the Sunne parched
them

them in the bloſſome; our harveſt being gotten in, our Governour ſent foure men on fowling, that ſo we might after
a more ſpeciall manner reioyce together, after we had gathered the fruit of our labours; they foure in one day killed
as much fowle, as with a little helpe beſide, ſerved the Company almoſt a weeke, at which time amongſt other Recrea-
tions, we exerciſed our Armes, many of the *Indians* cōming
amongſt vs, and amongſt the reſt their greateſt King *Maſſaſoyt*, with ſome nintie men, whom for three dayes we entertained and feaſted, and they went out and killed fiue Deere,
which they brought to the Plantation and beſtowed on our
Governour, and vpon the Captaine, and others. And although it be not alwayes ſo plentifull, as it was at this time
with vs, yet by the goodneſſe of God, we are ſo farre from
want, that we often wiſh you partakers of our plentie. Wee
haue found the *Indians* very faithfull in their Covenant of
Peace with vs; very louing and readie to pleaſure vs: we often goe to them, and they come to vs; ſome of vs haue bin
fiftie myles by Land in the Country with them; the occaſions
and Relations whereof, you ſhall vndeſtand by our generall
and more full Declaration of ſuch things as are worth the
noting, yea, it hath pleaſed God ſo to poſſeſſe the *Indians*
with a feare of vs, and loue vnto vs, that not onely the greateſt King amongſt them called *Maſſaſoyt*, but alſo all the
Princes and peoples round about vs, haue either made ſute
vnto vs, or beene glad of any occaſion to make peace with
vs, ſo that ſeauen of them at once haue ſent their meſſengers
to vs to that end, yea, an Fle at ſea, which we neuer ſaw hath
alſo together with the former yeelded willingly to be vnder
the protection, and ſubiects to our ſoueraigne Lord King
IAMES, ſo that there is now great peace amongſt the *Indians*
themſelues, which was not formerly, neither would haue bin
but for vs; and we for our parts walke as peaceably and
ſafely in the wood, as in the hie-wayes in *England*, we entertaine them familiarly in our houſes, and they as friendly be-
ſtowing their Veniſon on vs. They are a people without
any Religion, or knowledge of any God, yet very truſtie,

quicke of apprehenfion, ripe witted, iuft, the men and women goe naked, onely a skin about their middles; for the
temper of the ayre, here it agreeth well with that in *England*,
and if there be any difference at all, this is fomewhat hotter in
Summer, fome thinke it to be colder in Winter, but I cannot out of experience fo fay; the ayre is very cleere and not
foggie, as hath beene reported. I neuer in my life remember
a more feafonable yeare, then we haue here enioyed: and if
we haue once but Kine, Horfes, and Sheepe, I make no que-
ftion, but men might liue as contented here, as in any part of
the world. For fifh and fowle, we haue great abundance, frefh
Codd in the Summer is but courfe meat with vs, our Bay is
full of Lobfters all the Summer, and affordeth varietie of o-
ther Fifh; in September we can take a Hogfhead of Eeles in
a night, with fmall labour, & can dig them out of their beds,
all the Winter we haue Muffells and Othus at our doores:
Oyfters we haue none neere, but we can haue them brought
by the *Indians* when we will; all the Spring time the earth
fendeth forth naturally very good Sallet Herbs: here are
Grapes, white and red, and very fweete and ftrong alfo.
Strawberies, Goofeberies, Rafpas, &c. Plums of three forts,
with blacke and red, being almoft as good as a Damfen: a-
bundance of Rofes, white, red, and damask: fingle, but very
fweet indeed; the Countrey wanteth onely induftrious men
to imploy, for it would grieue your hearts (if as I) you had
feene fo many myles together by goodly Riuers vninhabited, and withall to confider thofe parts of the world wherein you liue, to be euen greatly burthened with abundance of
people. Thefe things I thought good to let you vnderftand,
being the truth of things as nere as I could experimentally
take knowledge of, and that you might on our behalfe giue
God thankes who hath delt fo fauourably with vs.

Our fupply of men from you came the ninth of *Nouember*
1 6 2 1. putting in at Cape Cod, fome eight or ten leagues
from vs, the *Indians* that dwell thereabout were they who
were owners of the Corne which we found in Caues, for
which we haue giuen them full content, and are in great
                                                    league

league with them, they sent vs word there was a ship nere
vnto them, but thought it to be a French man, and indeede
for our selues, we expected not a friend so soone. But when
we perceived that she made for our Bay, the Gouernor com-
manded a great Peece to be shot off, to call home such as were
abroad at worke ; whereupon euery man, yea, boy that
could handle a Gun were readie, with full resolution, that if
she were an Enemy, we would stand in our iust defence, not
fearing them, but God provided better for vs then we supposed ; these came all in health vnto vs, not any being sicke
by the way (otherwise then by Sea sicknesse) and so continue at this time, by the blessing of God, the good wife *Ford*
was deliuered of a sonne the first night shee landed, and both
of them are very well. When it pleaseth God, we are setled
and fitted for the fishing busines, and other trading, I doubt
not but by the blessing of God, the gayne will giue content
to all ; in the meane time, that we haue gotten we haue sent
by this ship, and though it be not much, yet it will witnesse
for vs, that we haue not beene idle, considering the small-
nesse of our number all this Summer. We hope the Mar-
chants will accept of it, and be incouraged to furnish vs
with things needfull for further imployment, which will
also incourage vs to put forth our selues to the vttermost.
Now because I expect your comming vnto vs with other of
our friends, whose companie we much desire, I thought
good to aduertise you of a few things needfull ; be carefull
to haue a very good bread-roome to put your Biskets in,
let your Cask for Beere and Water be Iron-bound for the
first tyre if not more ; let not your meat be drie salted, none
can better doe it then the Saylers ; let your meale be so hard
trodd in your Cask that you shall need an Ads or Hatchet
to worke it out with : Trust not too much on vs for Corne
at this time, for by reason of this last company that came,
depending wholy vpon vs, we shall haue little enough till
haruest ; be carefull to come by some of your meale to spend
by the way, it will much refresh you, build your Cabbins as
open as you can, and bring good store of clothes, and bed-
                                                    ing

ing with you; bring euery man a Musket or fowling Peece,
let your Peece be long in the barrell,and feare not the waight
of it, for moſt of our ſhooting is from Stands; bring iuyce
of Lemons,and take it faſting,it is of good vſe; for hot waters,Anni-ſeed water is the beſt, but vſe it ſparingly : if you
bring any thing for comfort in the Country, Butter or Sallet oyle,or both is very good; our *Indian* Corne even the
courſeſt,maketh as pleaſant meat as Rice,therefore ſpare that
vnleſſe to ſpend by the way; bring Paper, and Linced oyle
for your Windowes, with Cotton yarne for your Lamps;
let your ſhott be moſt for bigge Fowles, and bring ſtore of
Powder and ſhot : I forbeare further to write for the preſent, hoping to ſee you by the next returne, ſo I take my
leaue, commending you to the L O R D for a ſafe conduct
vnto vs. Reſting in him

Plimmouth in *New-England*
this 11.of December.
1 6 2 1.

Your louing Friend

E. W.

REASONS

Reasons & considerations touching
the lawfulnesse of remouing out of
England into the parts of *America*.

Orasmuch as many exceptions are daily made The Pream against the going into, and inhabiting of for- ble. raine desert places, to the hinderances of plantations abroad, and the increase of distractions at home : It is not amisse that some which haue beene eare witnesses of the exceptions made, and are either Agents or Abettors of such remoualls and plantations, doe seeke to giue content to the world, in all things that possibly they can.

And although the most of the opposites are such as either dreame of raising their fortunes here, to that then which there is nothing more vnlike, or such as affecting their home-borne countrey so vehemently, as that they had rather with all their friends begge, yea starue in it, then vndergoe a little difficultie in seeking abroad ; yet are there some who out of doubt in tendernesse of conscience, and feare to offend God by running before they be called, are straitned and doe straiten others, from going to forraine plantations.

For whose cause especially, I haue beene drawne out of my good affection to them, to publish some reasons that might giue them content and satisfaction, and also stay and stop the wilfull and wittie cauiller : and herein I trust I shall not be blamed of any godly wise, though thorow my slender iudgement I should misse the marke, and not strike the naile on the head, considering it is the first attempt that hath beene made (that I know of) to defend those enterprises. Reason would therefore, that if any man of deeper reach and better iudgement see further or otherwise, that he rather instruct me, then deride me.

And being studious for breuitie, we must first consider, Cautions. that whereas God of old did call and summon our Fathers *Gen.* 12. 1, 2. by predictions, dreames, visions, and certaine illuminations & 35. 1.

L to

Mat. 2. 19.
Pſal. 105. 13.
to goe from their countries, places and habitations, to reſide and dwell here or there, and to wander vp and downe from citie to citie, and Land to Land, according to his will and pleaſure. Now there is no ſuch calling to be expected for a-ny matter whatſoeuer, neither muſt any ſo much as imagine
Heb. 1. 1, 2.
that there will now be any ſuch thing. God did once ſo traine vp his people, but now he doth not, but ſpeakes in another manner, and ſo we muſt apply our ſelues to Gods preſent dealing, and not to his wonted dealing : and as the miracle
Ioſh. 5. 12.
of giuing Manna ceaſed, when the fruits of the land became plentie, ſo God hauing ſuch a plentifull ſtorehouſe of di-rections in his holy word, there muſt not now any extraordi-narie reuelations be expected.

But now the ordinarie examples and precepts of the Scriptures reaſonably and rightly vnderſtood and applied, muſt be the voice and word, that muſt call vs, preſſe vs, and direct vs in euery action.

Neither is there any land or poſſeſſion now, like vnto the
Gen. 17. 8.
poſſeſſion which the Iewes had in Caanan, being legally ho-ly and appropriated vnto a holy people the ſeed of Abra-ham, in which they dwelt ſecurely, and had their daies pro-longed, it being by an immediate voice ſaid, that he (the Lord) gaue it them as a land of reſt after their wearie trauels, and a type of Eternall reſt in heauen, but now there is no land of that Sanctimonie, no land ſo appropriated; none ty-picall : much leſſe any that can be ſaid to be giuen of God to any nation as was Canaan, which they and their ſeed muſt dwell in, till God ſendeth vpon them ſword or captiuitie : but now we are all in all places ſtrangers and Pilgrims, trauellers and ſoiourners, moſt properly, hauing no dwelling but in
2 Cor. 5. 1, 2, 3.
this earthen Tabernacle; our dwelling is but a wandring, and our abiding but as a fleeting, and in a word our home is
So were the Iewes, but yet their temporall bleſſings and in inſtances were more large then ours
no where, but in the heauens: in that houſe not made with hands, whoſe maker and builder is God, and to which all aſcend that loue the comming of our Lord Ieſus.

Though then, there may be reaſons to perſwade a man to liue in this or that land, yet there cannot be the ſame reaſons which the Iewes had, but now as naturall, ciuill and Religious
bands

hands tie men, so they muſt be bound, and as good reaſons for things terrene and heauenly appeare,ſo they muſt be led. And ſo here falleth in our queſtion, how a man that is here borne and bred, and hath liued ſome yeares, may remoue himſelfe into another countrie. *Obiect.*

I anſwer, a man muſt not reſpect only to liue, and doe good to himſelfe, but he ſhould ſee where he can liue to doe moſt good to others : for as one ſaith, *He whoſe liuing is but for himſelfe, it is time he were dead.* Some men there are who of neceſſitie muſt here liue, as being tied to duties either to Church, Common-wealth, houſhold, kindred, &c. but others, and that many, who doe no good in none of thoſe nor can doe none, as being not able, or not in fauour, or as wanting opportunitie, and liue as outcaſts : no bodies, eie-ſores, eating but for themſelues, teaching but themſelues, and doing good to none, either in ſoule or body, and ſo paſſe ouer daies, yeares, and moneths, yea ſo liue and ſo die. Now ſuch ſhould lift vp their eies and ſee whether there be not ſome other place and countrie to which they may goe to doe good and haue vſe towards others of that knowledge, wiſdome, humanitie, reaſon, ſtrength, skill, facultie, &c. which God hath giuen them for the ſeruice of others and his owne glory. *Anſw.* 1 What perſons may hence remoue. 2 Why they ſhould remoue.

But not to paſſe the bounds of modeſtie ſo far as to name any, though I confeſſe I know many, who ſit here ſtill with their talent in a napkin, hauing notable endowments both of body and minde, and might doe great good if they were in ſome places, which here doe none, nor can doe none, and yet through fleſhly feare, niceneſſe, ſtraitneſſe of heart, &c. ſit ſtill and looke on, and will not hazard a dram of health, nor a day of pleaſure, nor an houre of reſt to further the knowledge and ſaluation of the ſons of *Adam* in that *New world,* where a drop of the knowledge of Chriſt is moſt precious, which is here not ſet by. Now what ſhall we ſay to ſuch a profeſſion of Chriſt, to which is ioyned no more deniall of a mans ſelfe ? But ſome will ſay, what right haue I to goe liue in the heathens countrie ? *Luk.*19.20. *Reaſ.* 1. *Obiect.*

Letting paſſe the ancient diſcoueries, contracts and agreements which our Engliſh men haue long ſince made in thoſe *Anſw.*

parts,

parts, together with the acknowledgement of the histories and Chronicles of other nations, who professe the land of *America* from the Cape *De Florida* vnto the Bay of *Canado* (which is South and North 300. leagues and vpwards; and East and West, further then yet hath beene discouered) is proper to the King of England, yet letting that passe, lest I be thought to meddle further then it concerns me, or further then I haue discerning: I will mention such things as are within my reach, knowledge, sight and practise, since I haue trauailed in these affaires.

And first seeing we daily pray for the conuersion of the heathens, we must consider whether there be not some ordinary meanes, and course for vs to take to conuert them, or whether praier for them be only referred to Gods extraordinarie worke from heauen. Now it seemeth vnto me that we ought also to endeuour and vse the meanes to conuert them, and the meanes cannot be vsed vnlesse we goe to them or they come to vs: to vs they cannot come, our land is full: to them we may goe, their land is emptie.

This then is a sufficient reason to proue our going thither to liue, lawfull: their land is spatious and void, & there are few and doe but run ouer the grasse, as doe also the Foxes and wilde beasts: they are not industrious, neither haue art, science, skill or facultie to vse either the land or the commodities of it, but all spoiles, rots, and is marred for want of manuring, gathering, ordering, &c. As the ancient Patriarkes therefore remoued from straiter places into more roomthy, where the Land lay idle and waste, and none vsed it, though there dwelt inhabitants by them, as *Gen.* 13.6.11.12. and 34. 21. and 41.20. so is it lawfull now to take a land which none vseth, and make vse of it.

And as it is a common land or vnused, & vndressed countrey; so we haue it by common consent, composition and agreement, which agreement is double: First the Imperial Gouernor *Massasoit*, whose circuits in likelihood are larger then *England* and *Scotland*, hath acknowledged the Kings Maiestie of *England* to be his Master and Commander; and that once in my hearing, yea and in writing, vnder his hand to

Captaine

Captaine *Standish*, both he and many other Kings which are vnder him, as *Pamet*, *Nauset*, *Cummaquid*, *Narrowhiggonset*, *Namaschet*, &c. with diuers others that dwell about the baies of *Patuxet*, and *Massachuset*: neither hath this beene accomplished by threats and blowes, or shaking of sword, and found of trumpet, for as our facultie that way is small, and our strength lesse: so our warring with them is after another manner, namely by friendly vsage, loue, peace, honest and iust cariages, good counsell, &c. that so we and they may not only liue in peace in that land, and they yeeld subiection to *Psal.*110.3. an earthly Prince, but that as voluntaries they may be per- & 48. 3. swaded at length to embrace the Prince of peace Christ Iesus, and rest in peace with him for euer.

Secondly, this composition is also more particular and applicatorie, as touching our selues there inhabiting: the Emperour by a ioynt consent, hath promised and appointed vs to liue at peace, where we will in all his dominions, taking what place we will, and as much land as we will, and bringing as many people as we will, and that for these two causes. First, because we are the seruants of *Iames* King of *England*, whose the land (as he confesseth) is, 2. because he hath found vs iust, honest, kinde and peaceable, and so loues our company; yea, and that in these things there is no dissimulation on his part, nor feare of breach (except our securitie ingender in them some vnthought of trecherie, or our vnciuilitie prouoke them to anger) is most plaine in other Relations, which shew that the things they did were more out of loue then out of feare.

It being then first a vast and emptie *Chaos*: Secondly acknowledged the right of our Soueraigne King: Thirdly, by a peaceable composition in part possessed of diuers of his louing subiects, I see not who can doubt or call in question the lawfulnesse of inhabiting or dwelling there, but that it may be as lawfull for such as are not tied vpon some speciall occasion here, to liue there as well as here, yea, and as the enterprise is weightie and difficult, so the honour is more worthy, to plant a rude wildernesse, to enlarge the honour and fame of our dread Soueraigne, but chiefly to displaie the

efficacie

efficacie & power of the Gospell both in zealous preaching, professing, and wise walking vnder it, before the faces of these poore blinde Infidels.

As for such as obiect the tediousnesse of the voyage thither, the danger of Pirats robberie, of the sauages trecherie, &c. these are but Lyons in the way, and it were well for such men if they were in heauen, for who can shew them a place in this world where iniquitie shall not compasse them at the heeles, and where they shall haue a day without griefe, or a lease of life for a moment ; and who can tell but God, what dangers may lie at our doores, euen in our natiue countrie, or what plots may be abroad, or when God will cause our sunne to goe downe at noone daies, and in the midst of our peace and securitie, lay vpon vs some lasting scourge for our so long neglect and contempt of his most glorious Gospell.

Prou. 22. 13.

Psal. 49. 5.
Mat. 6. 34.

Amos 8. 9.

Ob.

But we haue here great peace, plentie of the Gospell, and many sweet delights and varietie of comforts.

Answ.
2 Chro. 32. 25.

True indeed, and farre be it from vs to denie and diminish the least of these mercies, but haue we rendered vnto God thankfull obedience for this long peace, whilst other peoples haue beene at wars? haue we not rather murmured, repined, and fallen at iars amongst our selues, whilst our peace hath lasted with forraigne power? was there euer more suits in law, more enuie, contempt and reproch then now adaies? *Abraham* and *Lot* departed asunder when there fell a breach betwixt them, which was occasioned by the straightnesse of the land : and surely I am perswaded, that howsoeuer the frailties of men are principall in all contentions, yet the straitnes of the place is such, as each man is faine to plucke his meanes as it were out of his neighbours throat, there is such pressing and oppressing in towne and countrie, about Farmes, trades, traffique, &c. so as a man can hardly any where set vp a trade but he shall pull downe two of his neighbours.

Gen. 13. 9. 10.

The Townes abound with young tradef-men, and the Hospitals are full of the Auncient, the country is replenished with new Farmers, and the Almef-houses are filled with old Labourers, many there are who get their liuing with bearing burdens, but moe are faine to burden the land with their

whole

whole bodies: multitudes get their meanes of life by prating, and so doe numbers more by begging. Neither come these straits vpon men alwaies through intemperancy, ill husbandry, indiscretion, &c. as some thinke, but euen the most wise, sober, and discreet men, goe often to the wall, when they haue done their best, wherein as Gods prouidence swaieth all, so it is easie to see, that the straitnesse of the place hauing in it so many strait hearts, cannot but produce such effects more and more, so as euery indifferent minded man should be ready to say with Father *Abraham, Take thou the right hand, and I will take the left* : Let vs not thus oppresse, straiten, and afflict one another, but seeing there is a spatious Land, the way to which is thorow the sea, wee will end this difference in a day.

That I speake nothing about the bitter contention that hath beene about Religion, by writing, disputing, and inueighing earnestly one against another, the heat of which zeale if it were turned against the rude barbarisme of the Heathens, it might doe more good in a day, then it hath done here in many yeares. Neither of the little loue to the Gospell, and profit which is made by the Preachers in most places, which might easily driue the zealous to the Heathens who no doubt if they had but a drop of that knowledge which here flieth about the streetes, would be filled with exceeding great ioy and gladnesse, as that they would euen plucke the kingdome of heauen by violence, and take it as it were by force.

The greatest let that is yet behinde is the sweet fellowship **The last let.** of friends, and the satietie of bodily delights.

But can there be two neerer friends almost then *Abraham* and *Lot*, or then *Paul* and *Barnabas*, and yet vpon as little occasions as we haue beere, they departed asunder, two of them being Patriarches of the Church of old ; the other the Apostles of the Church which is new, and their couenants were such as it seemeth might binde as much as any couenant betweene men at this day, and yet to auoid greater inconueniences they departed asunder.

Neither must men take so much thought for the flesh, as not to

to be pleafed except they can pamper their bodies with varie-
ty of dainties. Nature is content with little, and health is
much endangered, by mixtures vpon the ftomach: The delights of the palate doe often inflame the vitall parts: as the
Iames 3.6. tongue fetteth a fire the whole body. Secondly, varieties here
are not common to all, but many good men are glad to fnap
at a cruft. The rent taker liues on fweet morfels, but the rent
payer eats a drie cruft often with watery eies: and it is nothing to fay what fome one of a hundreth hath, but what the
bulke, body and cominalty hath, which I warrant you is fhort
enough.

And they alfo which now liue fo fweetly, hardly will their
children attaine to that priuiledge, but fome circumuentor or
other will outftrip them, and make them fit in the duft, to
which men are brought in one age, but cannot get out of it
againe in 7. generations.

To conclude, without all partialitie, the prefent confump-
tion which groweth vpon vs here, whilft the land groaneth
vnder fo many clofe-fifted and vnmercifull men, being com-
pared with the eafineffe, plaineneffe and plentifulneffe in liuing in thofe remote places, may quickly perfwade any man
to a liking of this courfe, and to practife a remoual, which being done by honeft, godly and induftrious men, they fhall
there be right hartily welcome, but for other of diffolute and
prophane life, their roomes are better then their companies;
for if here where the Gofpell hath beene fo long and plentifully taught, they are yet frequent in fuch vices as the Hea-
then would fhame to fpeake of, what will they be when there
is leffe reftraint in word and deed? My onely fute to all men
is, that whether they liue there or here, they would learne to
vfe this world as they vfed it not, keeping faith and a good
confcience, both with God and men, that when the day of
account fhall come, they may come forth as good and fruitfull feruants, and freely be receiued, and enter into the ioy of
their mafter.

R. C.

FINIS.